FAST TRACK

NETWORKING

TURNING CONVERSATIONS INTO CONTACTS

Lucy Rosen With
Claudia Gryvatz Copquin

CAREER
PRESS

Franklin Lakes, N.J.

FAST TRACK NETWORKING
EDITED BY NICOLE FAHEY
TYPESET BY KARA KUMPEL

Printed in the U.S.A. by Courier

To order this title, please call toll-free 1-800-CAREER-1 (NJ and Canada: 201-848-0310) to order using VISA or MasterCard, or for further information on books from Career Press.

CAREER
PRESS

The Career Press, Inc., 3 Tice Road, PO Box 687,
Franklin Lakes, NJ 07417
www.careerpress.com

Library of Congress Cataloging-in-Publication Data

Rosen, Lucy.
    Fast track networking : turning conversations into contacts / by Lucy Rosen with Claudia Gryvatz Copquin.
        p. cm.
    Includes bibliographical references and index.
    ISBN 978-1-60163-121-3 – ISBN 978-1-60163-741-3 (ebook)
        1. Business networks. 2. Online social networks. I. Copquin, Claudia Gryvatz, 1961- II. Title.

HD69.S8R674 2010
650.1'3—dc22

2010008885

FASTTRACKNETWORKINGFASTTRACKNI
KNETWORKINGFASTTRACKNETWORKIN
KINGFASTRACKNETWORKINGFASTTRAC
RACKNETWORKINGFASTTRACKNETWORI
ORKINGFASTRACKNETWORKINGFAST
ASTTRACKNETWORKINGFASTRACKNETV
ETWORKINGFASTRACKNETWORKINGF
IGFASTTRACKNETWORKINGFASTTRACK
CKNETWORKINGFASTTRACKNETWORKI
RKINGFASTTRACKNETWORKINGFASTTR
TTRACKNETWORKINGFASTTRACKNETW
TWORKINGFASTTRACKNETWORKINGFA
GFASTTRACKNETWORKINGFASTTRACKN

Acknowledgments

Networking is about giving and there have been so many people in my life that have given me their time, their talent, their words of encouragement, and their friendship. To thank a few: Donna Drake, Kerry Gillick Goldberg, Terese Arenth, Mary Scott, Tina Dzuik, Christy Shae, Stephen Kear, Jennifer Urrezzio, Ira Krause, Steven Krauser, Dave Goldberg, Andrea Goldberg, Alison Berke Morano, Aliza Sherman, Jane Dixon, John King, Karen Dallago, Ruth Eisner, Tracey Gittere, Peter Goldsmith, John Kominicki, Hilary Hartung, Melissa Kane Connolly, Tommie Mihalik, Marie Prieto, Melinda Potcher.... And many more, including all the women who have ever been a part of Women on The Fast Track....

Thank you to my daughter Samantha, who has attended many events with me since she was little, and has eaten those rubber chicken dinners right along with the rest of them. Sam, who has often patiently waited for me to "finish work," understanding that I did what I had to do in order for us to do what we wanted to do! She is the best daughter I could ever ask for!

My mentor, my friend, my soul sister, Marcia, who told me that I could do anything I wanted to and had the talent to do so. Thank you Marcia for being a constant source of love and support in my life.

Ellen Linnemann, who has, over the years, written, edited, fixed, spruced up, and just plain created the words I wanted to say in the voice they needed to be said in. She is a true professional and an even truer friend.

Lindsay Doyle, who created the beautiful cover of this book and is a constant source of creativity in the agency and in the world. Lindsay, you make the world a more colorful place to live. Thank you.

Claudia, my coauthor, who jumped into this project without hesitation or reservation and worked so very hard to be sure that this book was the way it was meant to be.

My mom and dad, who I guess knew from the time I was really young, couldn't put me in a box and expect I would do anything the "normal" way. Thank you for letting me find my own way in the world. My sisters, Molly and Amy, who are, hands down, the very best sisters and best friends I could ever have.

Finally, thank you to Bob, who gave me financial freedom, among other things, that allowed me to free my mind of the worry about money and allowed me to take the time to make *Fast Track Networking- Turning Conversations Into Contacts* a reality. Thank you for believing in me.

Contents

Foreword

Everyone has someone to thank for their lucky breaks in life and I have to thank the author of this book, Lucy Rosen. Lucy single-handedly launched my career and I was not a paying client. I was at the receiving end of Lucy's networking prowess as a founding member of Women on the Fast Track, her international women's networking group. If you want to learn how to network to forward your own career and those of the people you come in contact with, this a book you'll want to study, highlight, and keep as a reference forever.

When I met Lucy, I was an ex-waitress/actress who had just discovered the life-changing technology of personal coaching. I had been a coaching client first and I was fired up to help others achieve the personal and business breakthroughs I had had after completing the first training program in the United States for certifying professional coaches. I joined Women on the Fast Track to expand my network. I had discovered that actors as clients were not going to make me a living, so I needed to meet business professionals and fast. Little did I know that I was about to meet the powerhouse who would change my life.

I remember the day. It was a rainy evening in Manhattan, and our loyal group of networkers came out in the rain to meet in a nice, corporate-office training room. As we went around the room re-introducing ourselves and our businesses, Lucy interrupted my elevator speech and asked me what I charged. At the time, in an unproven profession, I was only asking $150 a month to work with clients. Lucy stood up and said, "Sign me up. I'm going to give this thing a try for 90 days." Well, not only did I have a full-paying, ideal client, I had a "mouthpiece"! Lucy went on to rave about her experience, and during the next year, almost every member in our group became a client of mine. Not only that, but one of them did extremely well and stayed with me for a couple of years. Her success story was told in *Money* magazine in 2006 and my business shot through the roof to include book deals, speaking internationally, becoming the owner of a coaching company, and many honors and distinctions along the way. Media appearances have become the norm and I have to thank Lucy for that, too. It was Lucy who passed my name on to the editor of *Entrepreneur* magazine and a few others, which resulted in starting my role as a media perennial.

By now, you might be wondering what the point of becoming a great networker like the author is if it's only going to benefit someone else. I am only telling you one side of the story. To be a "Lucy" or a great networker is never without great reward. Lucy creates loyal friends and business associates. When she asked me to write this forward, the answer was "Of course!" and when you are a master networker who has collected a cadre of people who you have helped, the flow of goodness, favors, business opportunities, and help coming toward you is huge. There is no shortage when you give as much or more than you receive. You will see that in the many real-life networking success stories on these pages.

As a business owner who has coached hundreds, if not thousands, of men and women in executive and entrepreneurial positions, I am uniquely poised to comment from a broad perspective about the changes the world-of-work is undergoing as a result of the global recessionary economic events. We are in the process of an interesting shift in the core of how business is done. The ways of the past are past. Dominance and competition (often at any cost) is on hold. Collaboration, sustainability, and social consciousness are in.

In the current climate, it is becoming common to hear that the longevity of employment and business success will be dependent more and more on right-brain capabilities such as intuition, creativity, and connection with people. It is time for people to contribute their unique genius instead of trying to fit in as we have for decades. We'll need to know who has what particular talent to round out our teams and our initiatives. Left-brain skills, usually technical, such as work with numbers, executing transactions, and other functions, are being outsourced, making the people who do them less essential to the process. A generous business spirit and the ability to connect with people in effective ways will become increasingly more important as businesses get temporarily smaller instead of larger, and as people consequently are forced to work closer together in corporations. Many more people are choosing entrepreneurship as a route and they have to become very focused on building relationships. Networking is key.

Men have known for centuries that opening doors for each other benefits everyone, but even they will have something to learn from this book. Women, often generalized as being competitive with other women, will have to debunk that habit if current employment and entrepreneurial numbers are indicative of the future. More women have held onto their jobs during current times than men. Men *and* women will want to have a large network to tap. You will want to be able to reach out whenever you need to acquire information, expertise, mentoring, or fill a position in your company. That won't be easy if you had not been nurturing relationships along the way.

Your success creates another example of what's possible for other people like you. That may sound like a burden, but it's not. It's a privilege. As will it be a privilege for you to read this book and take in the wisdom that will shorten your learning curve and bring you results beyond your wildest imagination.

I wish you great success and a fulfilling ride.

—Laura Berman Fortgang, MCC, author of *The Little Book On Meaning*, *Now What? 90 Days to a New Life Direction*, *Living Your Best Life*, and *Take Yourself to the Top*.

Introduction

I don't remember the first time I put two people to-gether for the sole purpose of them "connecting" on a professional level. But although I may not recall the names and specifics of the very first people that I helped by making that all-important connection, the experience must have had a tremendous impact on me—because I've spent the last 25 years continuing to connect people whenever, wherever, and however I can.

Why would I go out of my way to do this? What could I possibly gain from spending time, energy, and effort making connections between two people? I didn't have a contract stating that I would receive money, goods, or fa-vors from my connections. I didn't request that they con-nect me if I connected them. Wasn't I spending valuable time, energy, and often resources that I could be spend-ing on my own business, my own career, and my own endeavors? That's no way to run a business. It's certainly not a way to get ahead. And it definitely wasn't the way to be successful in the competitive "Greed is Good" business climate of the 1980s—where getting ahead seemed to mean putting yourself first at all times. Or was it?

Absolutely, positively, 100 percent yes. Although I didn't know it back then, the time I spent introducing people I knew to each other—the lunches I orchestrated, the meetings I arranged, the events I brought people to (even when I would rather have not gone for my own immediate business needs)—was probably some of the best-spent time of my early career.

When I first started really networking, it was 1985. I had just moved to New York City from Albuquerque, New Mexico, where I had spent a couple of years working in a PR and marketing agency. I was 25 years old, motivated, confident...and had decided I would go to the Big Apple and conquer the world. I think most of my friends and family thought I would be back in six months. I knew otherwise. As 10, then 20 years passed, I was still there, having successfully built my business, and even my growing circle of friends, through the power of what I now know were the "nuances of networking."

So what would a 25-year-old young woman just starting out in the 1980s know about networking? At that point in my life, it wasn't as much about what I knew worked, as much as what I knew *wasn't* working for so many people (especially women) when it came to making new business contacts. And being 25 and idealistic, I set out to revolutionize the New York City business world—or at least change the way people were networking.

What was networking like in 1985? As an outsider trying to break into the Manhattan businessworld, I firmly believed it was my best shot at making some valuable contacts. But I also couldn't believe how few opportunities there really were, for businesswomen in particular, to network with other businesswomen. Sure, I'd heard of the glass ceiling, but I wasn't even getting through the glass door to talk to the people I wanted to meet. So I did whatever I could as a young woman just starting out. I went to just about every networking meeting that I could find (there were a handful of networking groups as well as the requisite business and professional organizations at the time), but I only knew a few people, and when I went to these meetings, I felt like a fish out of water. I'd stand there and watch dozens, sometimes hundreds, of people, all standing around talking to each other. I didn't know where to put myself. I had no idea who to talk to. In fact, most of the time it felt like I was at a junior high school dance, where "really wanting to ask that cute boy to dance" had evolved into "really wanting to introduce yourself to that successful-looking man holding court with four other successful-looking people." Eventually I figured out what I needed to do and slowly learned the art of walking up to people, introducing myself, learning about them and their business needs, and making the most of every event I attended.

It started just like that, a decision I made to really embrace networking, not just endure the process and watch others have the conversations and make the contacts. I did what I was supposed to do. I kept going to these events (even when I may not have always felt like it at the time) and I started meeting more and more people. With my growing cadre of newfound contacts, who often became friends, I started putting the people I now knew together, for *their* benefit. It just seemed like the right thing to do. My contacts were rapidly expanding. My fledgling marketing and public relations agency was starting to grow. All was well in my world—thanks, in good part, to the power of networking. Networking was working, but I knew there had to be a way to make it work even better.

Like a lot of good ideas, mine came to me kind of out of the blue—or, in my case, literally *under* a blue sky. One day, while sitting on the beach out on Long Island, I started thinking about the markets that my agency was working with and where my interests really were, and all signs pointed to the women entrepreneurial/business market. I had joined a couple of the women's business groups, I was sitting on a couple of small boards, I was involved in a couple of New York State Women in Business initiatives, and I realized I had built contacts with many businesswomen throughout the region. *How great would it be*, I thought, *if I could take women from one of my groups and introduce them to other women from another group, look for some synergy between them, and maybe start our own business group?* In fact, there were a number of women I had grown to know who would probably welcome the chance to meet with some of the amazing business professionals who I was meeting. The idea had promise.

When I started thinking about the type of networking events that I was attending, I knew I was onto something. Although I had indeed become a much more experienced (and successful) networker, there was one thing that the existing networking scene wasn't offering women like me and the many other women slowly, but surely, entering the networking circle. I didn't like the fact that when I met someone at an event, I really only had a few moments with him or her before I needed to move on and meet/talk to someone else. If I didn't take the initiative to follow up with this woman or man, it was pretty likely that I'd never see him or her again, and it was really tiring to take the time to meet people, then follow up, go for coffee/lunch/drinks...followed up by, of course, more follow-up. I wanted to take the time to get to know them more naturally. I wanted to take the time to find out who they were. I wanted to find out if there was anything I could do to help them, anyone I could possibly connect them with, or hear any ideas that they simply wanted to bounce around. For me, meeting at a one-hour event didn't cut it. And I was betting on the fact that it wasn't cutting it for many other businesswomen like me who were looking for a new way to make, keep—and nurture—the contacts that they knew could help them grow their businesses.

So, that day on the beach, I came up with an idea. If I created a networking group specifically for women— helping professional women connect with other professional women, in an environment conducive to building long-term, mutually beneficial working relationships— would women be interested? Would they join? Would they, too, learn how connecting other people can help not only the people they are helping, but themselves, too? Would they welcome the opportunity to meet with other like-minded women on a regular basis? And, most importantly, would they benefit from a networking group just for women?

They were interested, they did join, and my idea, Women on the Fast Track, moved full-steam ahead.

I found an attorney that I liked, an image consultant whom I had met who had chutzpah, and a new business coach (I think she was the only one in New York City at the time and she wrote the foreword in this book). There were a couple of other women I invited. I called them all and invited them to a conference room in an office that I borrowed, and I explained the concept of Women on the Fast Track. I told them I didn't think we should have speakers. I didn't think we should meet anywhere but a board room (positive thinking, forward thinking). I told them that if we could somehow come together as a group and represent each other out in the sometimes overwhelming New York City business arena, it would be great, because instead of just us doing it by ourselves, we would now have a group of women who were actively promoting each other and each other's businesses.

They *loved* the idea. In fact, they loved the idea so much, they started telling *other* women that they knew about the meeting, and women started asking to participate in our group as well. Although I know that this may seem kind of "been there/done that" in this day and age—where virtually every town, city, and community has at least one group that operates in this fashion, keep in mind that this was 1985. There were no groups like this for women in business. Women on the Fast Track offered something different, and I had done what I had set out to do: make networking work even better, especially for businesswomen who, during those early years, had few resources when it came to formal networking groups. Before long, we launched new groups and together, we grew—we grew our businesses, we grew our networks, we grew our contacts and it was amazing! Today, WoTFT continues with small groups of like-minded women meeting in conference rooms across the country—sharing ideas, resources, connections, inspiration, and business. The success stories that have come out of this organization are amazing, not only the countless stories of the businesses that have started and grown, but the hundreds of friendships that have bloomed and flourished. Women on the Fast Track has truly put so many women on the *right* track...and has helped more women than I could have ever imagined.

Of course, even though Women on the Fast Track had taken off, I didn't stop going to other networking events. I continued to go, continuing to connect people that needed to be connected, continuing to think beyond my own business and my own business needs, and my business and career flourished. I connected start-up fashion designers with established manufacturers; connected food company executives with food service distributors; connected medical professionals with other healthcare professionals who could help grow their practices. I connected one of my favorite hair salons/spas with one of the leading plastic surgery practices on Long Island, leading to a strategic partnership that offered clients a great series of presentations. And it isn't only businesses that I've been lending my connection skills to all these years. I've connected parents I'd meet on the sidelines at soccer games and at PTA meetings to others in the area that I thought might be able to help in whatever project they might have been involved in at the time. And, of course, what better connection could I have made than when I introduced one of the country's top coffee company executives with one of the New York metropolitan area's leading baked goods distribution company owners, leading to an unprecedented "coffee and cake" promotion that not only made news, but gained new customers for each company.

During the past 25 years, I've learned a lot about networking. I've learned what makes a really good net-worker, what makes a not-so-good networker—and what can make the wrong type of networking actually backfire (I've witnessed countless "bad networking" scenarios that probably did more harm than good for the participants). I've learned how to be at an event and actually feel com-fortable—and not feel as if I'm at that junior high school dance staring anxiously across the floor at the person I want to meet. I've learned the importance of growing my network, never letting it stagnate…and I've learned the importance of follow-up and how to follow up the right way. I've "danced" with the best, the worst, and all sorts in between. I've proven that six degrees of separation is really only two (three at the most), especially based on all the great people in my network on whom I can call—and do call—on a regular basis. I've learned why intimate net-working works best for me—and possibly for you. And, I've learned how to balance it all.

Fast Track Networking: Turning Conversations Into Contacts is a compilation of everything I've learned by doing, listening, trying, and experiencing. It's a book that will share with you how to start networking, why it works, who it works with…and how to work it. It's a book that will give you success stories, as well as some horror stories, about networking from some of the hard-est working, smartest, most successful entrepreneurs and business people in the United States today. It will give you the tips, tools, and techniques to start your own group if you choose, or how to find a group that fits you best. I hope it gives you the push you need to get out there and start your own inner circle of 10 (you'll learn what this is later on...) and develop your outer circle of networking contacts.

And just to give you a little more inspiration, I am sharing with you the following, which my mother sent to me in 1987. I don't know who wrote it, but it truly sums up how I feel about networking and what I believe it to be.

In fall, when you see geese heading south for the winter, flying along in V-formation, you might consider what science has discovered as to why they fly that way:

As each bird flaps its wings, it creates an uplift for the bird immediately following.

By flying in V-formation, the whole flock adds at least 71 percent greater flying range than if each bird flew on its own. (People who share a common direction and sense of community can get where they are going more quickly and easily because they are traveling on the thrust of one another.)

When a goose falls out of formation, it suddenly feels the drag and resistance of trying to go it alone, and quickly gets back into formation to take advantage of the lifting power of the bird in front. If we have as much sense as the goose, we will stay in formation with those who are headed the same way we are!

When the head goose gets tired, it rotates back in the wind and another goose flies point. It is sensible to take turns with people who are doing demanding jobs.

Finally, when a goose gets sick, or is wounded by gun-shot, and falls out of formation, two other geese fall out with that goose and follow it down to lend help and protection. They stay with the fallen goose until it is able to fly, or until it dies; only then do they launch out on their own, or with another formation to catch up with the group. (If we have the sense of a goose, we will stand by each other like that.)

People who share a common direction and sense of community can get where they are going more quickly and easily because they are traveling on the thrust of one another, and are committed to each other throughout the journey.

Be a goose. Find people who share your vision. Belong to a community. Commit to helping others in their quests, whatever that may be. I promise you, the payoff will be much greater than the effort.

To me, there is perhaps no better feeling than the one that you get when you know you've helped some-one—and that you've done it unconditionally, without expecting anything at all in return. It's what networking is all about...and it's why I do it day after day, year after year. My hope is that, after reading this book, you'll learn that networking really isn't about the business cards. It's not even really about growing your business, or filling a business need, in the short term. It's about building and nurturing the relationships that will, in effect, help you throughout your lifetime.

Here's hoping that your next conversation will turn into a valuable contact for all involved...and happy networking!

Chapter One
Networking Is Like Dating, Only Better

You feel a little flutter in your stomach as the time draws closer. You find yourself uncharacteristically apprehensive, giving everything the "once-over" checklist before you go out the door, making sure you've got the right outfit and the right frame of mind for what lies ahead. You've got your mental list of "conversation starters" and scintillating tidbits of current events trivia that you've been stockpiling for days—and can speak knowingly on topics ranging from hot issues in politics to the hottest restaurants in town. You're ready. You're armed. And, if you're like millions of other people, you're a little bit nervous.

Sound familiar? Everyone has felt this way at one time or another during the dating process. Many people feel those same exact "pre-date" jitters when venturing out to a networking event. Come to think of it, dating and networking are incredibly similar—and approaching the networking process like dating does more than make sense. It makes great *business* sense.

Whether dating is a distant memory for you, or whether you are currently navigating your way through today's dating pool, there are some really good reasons to approach networking like dating. And just like dating, you never know when that one date—or networking event—will turn out to be the one that will transform your life.

In this chapter, we will look at how similar dating and networking really are and how some simple dating strategies can be adapted for networking with amazing results. You'll learn why networking trumps dating, and how to set your own personal networking goals so that your "dating pool" (or circle of influence as I refer to it in the networking arena) continues to expand. We'll talk about the best places to meet new potential contacts and to reconnect with the ones you would like to know better. Plus, once we've addressed how you can enhance your networking savvy, we'll tell you how *you* can best play matchmaker for other potential networkers—and pay it forward with what you've learned.

Oh, to Be Carefree and Single

When you're single and dating, you may go out with just about everyone, and for good reason. After all, you and your next date may just click, and that click leads to another rendezvous. You grow mindful of this person's well-being, sharing information about events of interest. Soon enough, you start thinking of this special someone throughout the week, wondering how to make this person's life happier, easier, and more fulfilled. Along with romantic interest comes friendship and trust. With trust comes commitment, where both parties are determined to help each other out whenever and wherever possible.

It's the same with networking. You've got to meet a host of different people, and be willing to give a little. And you must be patient and understand that this effort is all about the relationship. Now, here's the downside. Just like dating, sometimes networking relationships don't take off either. And that's okay. As a mature adult, you won't simply discount the person who isn't a fit for you. Instead, you'll introduce him or her to another who is also part of the dating pool. Who knows? That person may be the perfect fit for someone else. But when it comes to networking, don't just share the "misfits." Make introductions all around—even if it means sharing your best contacts.

Good Things Come to Those Who…Share

Good networkers share their contacts altruistically. They are not looking for or expecting anything in return, other than perhaps some heartfelt appreciation that someone went out of his or her way to do something helpful. These good networkers know that somewhere down the line, they will receive the same courtesy—or maybe they already have, and understand the profound impact from an act of kindness, not to mention the boost it can give to a career track or profit line.

They may or may not see any kind of results right away, and that's okay. Lasting relationships are not built overnight. Trust and friendship take time, and the more seeds you plant, the more fruitful the rewards. Just ask Maxine Clark, the founder and "Chief Executive Bear" of Build-A-Bear Workshop in St. Louis, Missouri. "I believe that 1 + 1 = 10 and that the way to do that is [to] spread the opportunities," she points out. "Help others and they will help you. This has never backfired and has given me more opportunities."

These opportunities often come from the least likely resources. Take for example, the time when Build-A-Bear, a $487 million company, sought out a printer for a project on a tight deadline. Clark wondered if she'd have to scrap the entire project, given the short timeframe. But a friend shared a vendor that could help, and as Clark put it, "She didn't hesitate at all, even knowing our size might cannibalize her [relationship as] a smaller business with the printer." Summing it, Clark says, "I learned that even the smallest company can help a bigger company be successful. Again, 1 + 1 = 10. If that happens, we are all better!"

The more creative and proactive you are as a networker, the more likely it is that you will build relationships, especially when extending acts of kindness beyond the four walls of a networking event. Consider for example Scott Chazdon, who calls himself the "Doctor of Automotive Wellness" at Maintenance & More Automotive Specialists in Albuquerque, New Mexico. "I share contact lists with networking people all the time," Chazdon notes. "For doing business with ABC Cleaners, you can get a free oil change with my company. And for doing business with me, you can get this or that from them."

Of course, unlike Maxine Clark's friend, some may think they are treading dangerous waters when they start to reveal their best contacts. Not Ryan McCormick, president of Rising Sun PR, a boutique public relations firm in New York. "I feel that sharing your best contacts shows confidence because you're not afraid to lose anything," he says. "Sharing my best contacts with new people has led to new business and countless referrals because *no one* else will share their contacts—it makes you stand out."

Yes, there is always that chance that some will not reciprocate the favor, or worse, some may close in on your territory. Yes, there is always the chance that the new people you meet may like someone in your circle better than they like you. And yes, they may even do business together. After all, people generally cut deals with the people they like. They may share some or even all of their business referrals and information with others, rather than you. Get over it. As McCormick puts it: "Life is what it is. For every contact someone steals, I'll just meet twenty new ones and be sure not to do business with the stealer again."

Some chalk up these unfortunate episodes to experience, discovering a thing or two about a person's character that they would prefer to learn sooner rather than later. "I learn that they are people I can't truly trust and it is their loss," says Marcia Glenda Rosen, president of M. Rosen Consulting & Communications, a business development firm in Westhampton, New York. "I no longer bring them referrals or the many connections I have developed over the years. My connections are my center of influence, and I only want to bring people into my network that will respond appropriately."

So go ahead and play matchmaker. Share your contacts. In fact, share it all. But if somehow that generosity is not reciprocated to some degree, don't take it personally—and put aside any and all feelings of insecurity. Instead, recognize that it may be time to reconsider individual relationships with those who are not as giving as you are, and move forward (and keep sharing) with the many others out there who, like you, understand what networking is really all about. Network by example, and be a networker at every opportunity. You'll find that not only does sharing your resources make you a more successful networker, but it makes you a trusted, valuable contact for everyone you know. And that, of course, is what networking is really all about—and why those who share unconditionally find that they often get back just as much as they give. And then some.

Take It to the Next Level With a Plan

Suppose you are a natural networker. You tend to strike up conversations equally with executives at a business gathering or with other parents on the sidelines of the soccer field. You attend every social and professional event possible, knowing that each event is filled with promise. And along the way you are always thinking about how you can help others. You like to think about who you know that can help them, or what strategies they should try to get from point A to point B. Even if you were born with the gift to connect and assist others, you might be surprised that there is still so much more you can do when it comes to networking. What you need, though, is a plan.

Those who plan and set their networking goals find that they can indeed broaden their circles. Yet surprisingly few businesspeople—even the savvy ones—do this enough. The best way to get started? Take out a pen and paper and start to define your goals.

By defining your networking goals, you are taking a critical first step in building an effective association of people. Before you start identifying and listing out your goals, clarify in your own mind what you need or want. Simply saying "I want more business" will never be enough to achieve your goals. This may take a bit of research. Determine the industries in which you want to establish more relationships. Figure out who it is you need to meet to get there. Set up a realistic plan of what you can and *will* do to try to build these new relationships, not only by attending various networking events and business functions that you think they'll attend, but by putting in place a daily networking plan that will make networking and relationship-building part of your everyday routine.

Setting a goal of daily networking may seem intimidating, but the truth is, it's not. It all depends on how you view networking, and how you plan to approach making new connections. For those people who view networking as having to go, business-card-in-hand, to yet another networking function, doing this on a daily basis would seem not only an unattainable goal, but also pretty unpleasant. That's not what daily networking is all about.

What setting a plan for daily networking means—and why it's so important these days—is setting a plan to do something, every day, that is going to allow you to reach out to just one person that you might not have otherwise contacted. Maybe it's an old college friend or fraternity/sorority buddy. Maybe it's a former coworker from one of your first jobs, whom you've heard through the grapevine has risen through the ranks and is running his or her own successful company. Or maybe it's the person at the last networking meeting (or PTA meeting, for that matter) whom you heard was looking for advice about fundraising and who you can offer to either help or direct him or her to someone else who might be able to help with his or her immediate needs. Whoever it is, and whatever it takes, stick to your daily networking plan and I guarantee you'll see some amazing results from making just one call, and re-connecting with just one person a day.

Seven Best Tips for Setting Networking Goals

1. Be as clear and specific as possible in describing your goals. Saying that you want a new job, want more clients, or want to increase your business is not clear. But saying that you want a new job in a specific field, or even in a specific company, helps people know what to give you. Identifying what type of clients you want to work with and being able to explain to the people in your network what to listen for so that they think of you will help them refer more business to you. Everyone wants to increase their business! Are you able to identify what markets are the most appropriate markets or

industries to target in order to increase your business? The clearer you are, the more targeted you are, and the better it is for you!

2. Lay out your goals in the short term, which is month-by-month; long term, which would be the next year or two, and then future being within two to five years. Short-term goals can be as simple as attending three different organized networking groups and deciding which one to join, or calling two or more people that you haven't spoken to in the last six months and inviting them out for coffee, lunch, or just a quick business meeting. Long-term goals can be described as action items such as: obtaining a seat on the board of the not-for-profit that you are active in, or developing a workshop on your area of expertise and beginning to reach out to organizations, associations, groups, and gatherings in your community to pursue speaking in public (one of the best ways to not only market yourself but to meet new people). Future goals could include things like starting your own networking group, or working toward being further recognized as an expert in your industry.

3. Make sure your goals are realistically attainable within the designated time frame. Goals are great to have as they keep us focused, give us something to work toward, and motivate us. They can also be daunting, so if this is the first time you've developed goals for yourself, keep them simple, attainable, and make sure that after you identify a goal that you write a couple of action steps underneath

each so that you understand what it takes to reach that goal. Let's say one of your goals is that you want more press on you and your business. The action steps may be something like: determine the budget you can allocate for this activity; interview several public relations agencies that come recommended from people in your network; determine if you want to work with an agency, an individual, or if you want to try and do this yourself. Read books on creating press for yourself and your business, subscribe to a couple of online press newsletters, watch and listen to what others in your industry are doing, and so on. If each goal has a few action steps, it will keep you focused and be easier to follow. Goals should also be fluid, as they can change. You may think that one of your goals is to start a new division within your company, but after actively pursuing a couple of the action steps, such as researching the market to ascertain viability of starting this division, you find that the market is soft. If that's the case, change your goal! Be open to change. Be open to adjusting. Be flexible. That's the way you will get what you want.

4. Set up a daily networking plan and set daily goals, making sure to connect with someone each day that you can either help in some way, or who may be able to help you. Again, if you are clear on your goals and even clearer on the action steps it will take to reach your goals, you will have an easy time of setting up a daily networking plan and achieving your daily goals. One step at a time is a great way to pursue a goal and if you do one

thing every day that gets you closer to your goal, that's fabulous!

5. Make it one of your goals to have fun while networking, treating each event you go to as just a fun party with interesting guests. This will take the *work* out of networking! You may think you aren't going to like networking. You may already not like networking, but maybe you've gone about the entire process in a non-fun way. What would make it fun for you? Is it more fun for you to invite others to attend events with you? Then invite them! Is it more fun for you to volunteer in an active, large organization such as a Civitan Group, rather than attending industry networking events? It doesn't really matter where you network, as long as you do it. What could be more fun than making new friends? Most of the time, people don't have fun networking because they are stuck in that mindset that it's about getting, taking, or conquering, more business, more connections, and so on. Don't look at it that way. See it as developing relationships.

6. Review your goals monthly and adjust them as necessary. Keep your goal sheet out where it's visible so that it reminds you to do one pro-active networking activity per day. Don't just write out your goals and stick them in a drawer. Write them out, hang them up, and talk about them. And if you think you don't have time to do one proactive activity per day, you do. Send a quick e-mail to someone you just met with a link to something of interest within their industry. Cut out a newspaper article about business growth and success and

send it to the person you met three months ago who just started their own business. Call your ex coworker and ask him or her to meet you for coffee next week.

7. Be accountable to your goals. If you aren't great at being accountable, get an accountability partner. Hire a coach or someone who can review your goals with you and keep you accountable in the action steps necessary to reach your goals. Goals are only as good as the person working toward them, so if you are someone who makes lists upon lists of things you want to accomplish and never seem to get anywhere, you may find that having someone on your team or by your side to help you is a good idea. Yes, you may have to pay this person, but I guarantee you that if you are reading this book, you want more in your business life, so that probably means more money. And because you are going to get what you want, spend the money now to get you where you want to be. Invest in yourself—it is the best investment you'll ever make!

The Give and Take of Networking

Defining your networking goals is a critical first step toward building an effective network. You should be as clear and specific as possible in describing your goals then divide your list into short term (month-by-month) and future (two to five years) goals. Make sure your goals are realistically attainable within the designated time frame.

Before you can ask other people for help, you have to be clear in your own mind about what you need or want – just saying, "I want more business," is not enough to achieve your goals.

GOALS LIST

SHORT TERM

1.

2.

3.

4.

5.

LONG TERM

1.

2.

3.

4:

5.

Going Where the Networking Is Good

Those looking to grow their own potential know that good networking can be found anywhere...and everywhere. From the chicken dinner event, to a charity golf outing, to a gathering at a friend's beach house, there are probably dozens of opportunities every week for most people to network. And while they might not be the traditional "networking events" that you are used to, they can present even more of an opportunity to expand your own contact base and help others as well. So greet each party invitation, school function, and even airplane/train ride or vacation as an opportunity to perhaps make a new connection or form a new contact. It will add to the general fun of everyday life, and add volumes to your contact base.

Of course, in addition to everyday networking, the "networking event" remains a guaranteed-to-work tool for networkers of every level—and there are plenty of good networking events out there. In fact, it's relatively easy to find good networking events. In order to discover them, you'll just need to do some legwork. Read your local business paper and check out both its business events calendar and charitable events calendar. Mark the ones that seem intriguing or that speak directly to your goals and aspirations. Maybe a local association within your industry is holding a meeting in which you can find people that can help you brush up on skills. Or maybe a professional group is holding a conference that may attract the kinds of decision makers you would like to get to know. Join social networking groups such as LinkedIn, Twitter, and Facebook to build relationships with people online and find out where they are going and what they are doing to build their network. Social networking is perhaps the biggest thing to hit both old and new networkers in years—and we'll be taking a further, in-depth look at social networking in Chapter Ten.

Do Your Homework First

Before leaving home, smart networkers always do their homework. Prior to each event, they find out who will likely be in attendance, either by viewing an online RSVP list if it's available, or by actually contacting the organizer and asking who may be in the room during that event. But they don't stop there. Smart networkers take time before the event to research the names of the individuals they would like to get to know better. Armed with a few details about the people they'd like to meet, they are prepared with background and conversation tidbits, and are likely to not only make a good connection but a great *impression*, as well.

Doing a little research about an event or a group before attending does two things—it gets you excited about attending because you found out that it's either exactly where you need to go to meet the people you want to meet or not.

I get invitations all the time to attend parties, events, and group outings, and although I really want to attend all of them, I can't. I know that my business networking targets are other entrepreneurs, and other growth-oriented companies. Broken down even more, my targets are entrepreneurs and companies in specific industries. So how do I choose which events to attend? I choose by sometimes reaching out to the organizer and talking to them about what it is that they are looking for in terms of making their event successful. By asking them what their intentions are with their event, I can determine if their intentions meet my intentions. For example, if they tell me that they are gathering a group of people thinking about leaving corporate America to start their own companies, that this is a group intended for newbie entrepreneurs, then that's my market. That's a lot of my clients' market. That's a market I know well and can absolutely help the people attending by suggesting people for them to meet.

Your Personal Network

Even if you have yet to actively network, chances are you already have a foundation of people who you turn to when you need to know more about something, whether it's finding a new assistant who will go the extra mile for your company, finding a new vendor whose pricing is fair and quality is exceptional, or even purchasing a new car that gives great mileage. And in turn, more than likely you also are a good resource—a person others turn to when they need assistance, whether it is finding a reliable contractor, a great restaurant, or a reliable tax preparer.

Sit down, and make another list, this time identifying who you turn to, and who turns to you, in all facets of your life. By recognizing who you know from your past and current history, you will best be able to assess who would benefit by meeting new people.

Your Personal Network

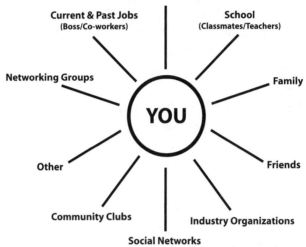

Current and Past Jobs (Boss/Co-workers)	Community Clubs	Family
_____	_____	_____
_____	_____	_____
_____	_____	_____

Networking Groups	Social Networks	School (Classmates/Teachers)
_____	_____	_____
_____	_____	_____
_____	_____	_____

Other	Industry Organizations	Religious Institutions
_____	_____	_____
_____	_____	_____
_____	_____	_____

Friends

_____
_____
_____

The people on your list make up your *personal network*. They are of great value to you in that they have proven themselves to be reliable resources. You can take this foundation a step further by creating your own networking events—and you don't even have to be a great organizer to do so. For example, invite a few of your contacts to meet you for lunch or coffee. Host a small dinner party at your home, or better still, invite the entire list of people over for a potluck. Not up to entertaining at home? Organize a meeting at a centrally located place. Ask your contacts to bring a friend. Now you—and your contacts—are expanding your circles two-, three-, and even four-fold.

When building your personal network, remember this: People generally want to do business with people they know and like. Creating and nurturing a strong personal network of people who not only know you but who know what you can do, and know that you're there to help, is perhaps one of the most important parts of successful networking. It's these people in your personal network, the ones who know what you do, what you know, and how your unique skill set can be of value to them and the people *they* know, who can increase your business by leaps and bounds. Be sure, though, that everyone in your personal network truly understands not only what you do, but how great you are at what you do. Your personal network can be your chief allies, your biggest cheerleaders, and your most valued relationships. Nurture them, value them, and help *them* as much as they help you.

Tips for Nurturing Your Personal Network

- **Quantity vs. Quality.** Like most things in life, it's not quantity as much as quality when it comes to a powerful personal network. Your personal network is really comprised of those people in your "inner circle" who you not only trust with your reputation, but who you would also bet your reputation on, and who share your sense of personal responsibility and commitment to helping others.

- **Make sure everyone in your personal network knows exactly what you do.** Fine-tune your 30-second "elevator pitch" (a brief description about yourself), and use it, even if you've known someone for years.

- **Listen.** Make sure you're not the only one doing the talking when you get together with those in your personal network. Keep an ear open for something that might spark an idea as to how you can help and ask questions that show your sincere interest in what they do.

- **Do someone a favor—no strings attached.** They'll not only value the help you've provided, but they'll value your relationship, and generosity, even more.

As a Fast Track Networker, You Now Know:

- When dating, there are some dates that just "click" while others just don't. The same holds true for networking. And just as we've all probably cringed when seeing the quintessential "bad first date" couple out at a restaurant, with seemingly nothing to say and no chemistry in the air whatsoever, watching (or being a part of) an awkward networking exchange can be equally uncomfortable.

- View a networking event as just a party with interesting guests. Don't expect anything from the event other than the chance to meet and mingle with new people.

- Speak to everyone at the party and take the time to introduce them to others.

- The best networkers are not only happy to make new contacts, but are equally as happy to share their contacts.

- Set specific networking goals before attending networking events, as this will help you determine which events you should go to. It will also help you take action on a daily basis to help someone else.

- Most importantly, never get discouraged or jaded, and always look toward the next networking event (or date) as the one that just may change your life (or at least career) forever.

It may seem counter-intuitive, but I really enjoy sharing my contacts with others. Even if nothing at all comes of the connections, it just makes you feel good to do for others, and really, it doesn't require much effort.

—Becky Kingsbury,
president, National Sales Associates
Winter Springs, Florida

Chapter Two
Get the Party Started

If you're a gregarious person who looks forward to social events, loves meeting, conversing, and sharing with new people, and have a keen, innate ability to work a room, then congratulations. You're a perfect candidate for any and all types of networking events. But let's be a bit more realistic and address the far more common scenario: For those who are a bit shy, as well as the many brilliant businesspeople out there that are actually quite introverted and bashful, I can think of few situations that appear more intimidating than entering a roomful of people at a gathering. The prospect can be so daunting that it prohibits many businesspeople from ever attending networking events at all. And that's truly a shame—for all people involved.

Overcoming Timidity

If you are someone who really gets scared or uncomfortable with the prospect of being in a networking situation, there are ways to help yourself. One would be to hire a business coach to talk through the issues you may have when it comes to socializing on a business level. In this day and age, not being able to represent yourself well in a social forum is a huge detriment to yourself and to your business; that is, unless all of your business is done over the Internet and you never have to talk to anyone in person. But let's be real—how often is that the case? I can't think of any business model that requires no direct contact with other people, ever!

Another way to overcome your shyness is to take miniscule networking steps by trying out groups and events that are relatively small. This will make the idea of meeting just a few strangers (rather than a roomful) much more manageable. And while I always encourage networkers to get out there and meet others, if you are really introverted, it's perfectly fine to just survey what's going on and wait until you see someone you may want to talk to, or wait for someone to say hello to you. After attending a few events like this as an observer, you will likely start feeling a bit more comfortable because you'll know exactly what to anticipate. You will also become a familiar face to those who network at these events regularly, which will prompt others to greet you and draw you into conversation.

And here's another good tip: if you are super uncomfortable about initiating conversations, wearing something that might attract attention might make it easy for people in attendance to start up a conversation with you. If you're a woman, try an interesting brooch, scarf, or necklace, or a brightly colored jacket or blouse. If it's unusual, people are likely to comment to break the ice. A unique (yet still business appropriate) tie or bowtie should do the trick if you're a man.

Of course, since you are reading this book, whether you are extremely introverted or not, you recognize the value in networking and have the desire to learn how to do it effectively. So let's say you are a little shy, ready to give networking your best effort, yet you still have reservations. You are not alone. I know many people who wish they were networking, but offer the following gripes (or excuses!) for not doing more of it. Among them:

- "I often get the feeling that new people I meet at these events might not necessarily be interested in what I do."
- "When I enter a networking event, it seems as though everyone there already knows each other and I'm the only stranger."
- "I never know who to talk to first."
- "I have difficulty starting conversations with strangers."
- "Because people are already conversing, I feel as though I'd be interrupting them to introduce myself, so I just don't do it."

These are all valid issues, although for the most part, incorrect assessments of networking situations. Let's take for example the first complaint. *"I often get the feeling attendees might not necessarily be interested in what I do."*

Grasping Your Value

In a nutshell, it's not about what you do. Most novice networkers think that if they are going to a networking event, it's about them: who can they meet, what can they accomplish for their own business. Instead, think of networking as a way to help others—connecting others with people that you know who might be beneficial to their business goals. So it's not at all about what you do, but who you might know. Do you coach a Little League team? Do you sing in a church choir? Are you involved in the PTA? Do you sit on a board of a not-for-profit? Look at all the people you know! If you feel as though you are only your "job"—what you do—then you are right; it sure is going to be uncomfortable (and downright boring for anyone you're talking to). But if you can feel as though you are a walking Rolodex, a person who has a number of different contacts from different avenues of your life, then you can also understand the value you bring to a gathering. You are now able to listen when people talk about what *they* do and put two and two together. By maintaining this mindset, you are going to be eager to attend many events. More importantly, though, people are going to be eager to meet, and get to know you.

Roomful of Strangers

Networking, when done right, is a mutually beneficial working relationship. When you understand that, you may be able to think more closely about your initial concerns about entering a networking event and feeling as if you're the only stranger, or the "odd man out" in a room full of people who already know each other. It's quite possible that some people do already know each other at local networking events. Smart businesspeople tend to fully recognize the benefits of connecting by networking and attend many events where they often run into each other. What this means to you is that the more networking events you go to, the greater the chances that eventually you will also know many people there, as well. So, given time (and future appearances at as many networking events as you can), you'll no longer feel like an outsider, and not only will you be on the networking fast-track, but you'll find yourself on the networking *inside* track.

Suppose this is your first event and it appears that everyone in the room is already engaged in a conversation (a likely scenario, as that is the purpose of the event). Chances are, there are also many strangers within the group, although they may not be as readily apparent on the surface, and you may have to seek them out during the course of the event. Networking event organizers understand the value of inviting a variety of guests to these events, so the networking opportunities remain fresh, and there are always new people to exchange information with.

There is a very simple way to overcome the feeling that you are an outsider among a group of insiders—invite a colleague or friend to attend the event with you. If you can't arrive together, plan on meeting just outside the venue, so you can walk in together. Now your entrance is not as intimidating, you have someone to talk to as you warm up to the occasion, and your friend may know a guest or two, which will facilitate introductions and conversations. Remember, you are there to meet others, so make a plan ahead of time to separate, mingle, and each meet a certain number of people. You can even make it a game and compare notes at the end of the evening.

Avoid Being Fashionably Late

Arriving to networking functions fashionably late will work against you if you find these events intimidating. As mentioned earlier, if you are not accustomed to making an entrance, there may be nothing more frightening than stepping into a crowded, buzzing room. So instead, arrive just right on time or, better yet, a bit early. This will give you a great advantage: you will now be in a position to observe who is walking into the event, and to make mental notes as you see faces you recognize. Being one of the first to arrive can also give you the appearance of being a host—provided you are not standing inconspicuously at the back of the room, of course!

Sometimes It's Not Who You Know…It's Where You Stand

Placing yourself at the rear of the room, by the restrooms, or in a corner will not serve you well in a networking scenario and, in fact, can actually do you more harm than if you stayed at home. You'll look like you don't want to be there or, worse yet, like you aren't confident enough to strike up a conversation with anyone. The preferable spot is by the entrance, so you can greet people as they enter. This is not to say you should overshadow the actual hosts of the event, but rather, position yourself so that you are able to extend a greeting to anyone that passes you. By acting like a host/hostess, rather than being a passive guest, you put yourself in control of the experience. More importantly, you will be perceived as someone in the know, someone who is confident, and someone that other guests want to meet.

If you go to an event with the purpose of making sure everyone there has a good time and connects with the people they need to connect with, you will feel a sense of not just importance, but that you are there to be sure others' needs are met. This oftentimes makes someone who doesn't feel comfortable going to an event feel good about going. And knowing that you are there to help others—in addition to helping yourself—not only alleviates some of the "networking pressure" that you might feel prior to a networking event, but allows you to leave each event knowing that, whether or not you made a new contact for yourself, your time was well spent.

No Selling Allowed

One thing that you need to avoid at all costs during any type of networking event is selling. There's a time and a place for everything, but a full-force, going-in-for-the-kill selling of yourself, your company, and/or your services at a networking event is definitely the wrong approach.

Networking is all about helping others achieve their goals. So rather than approaching the evening's event as a way to increase your business, consider it an ideal opportunity to form new relationships so you can help others. Believe it or not, this tactic takes the pressure off you for the night. Now you can move about the room freely, without the burden of feeling as though you are there to drum up business.

Start the Conversation

Everyone who attends a networking event is there for the same reason: to engage in some really great conversations that can possibly open the door to a new connection or future business relationship. So if everyone is there to engage in conversations, why do so many people have trouble starting one up? And what are some of the best ways to take charge of the situation, lose the awkwardness, and get the ball rolling by starting the conversation yourself?

It's common knowledge that many people, even those who appear to be the most confident, and who may be running multi-million dollar companies, find it awkward to introduce themselves and get a conversation started. So it's up to you to be in charge by making the first move. Extend your hand, offer a warm greeting and you'll note that before long, it won't seem like networking. It will seem like just a great conversation with a new, and potentially interesting, individual. And while you'll be happy (and relieved) to have started up a conversation, chances are that the person you're talking to will be equally as happy to be involved in a meaningful conversation.

As you become a more seasoned networker, you'll find that taking the lead will become second nature. In addition, you'll find that there are a number of different, and effective, ways to strike up a conversation at a networking function, and you will learn which style(s) fit your personality best. Roshini Rajkumar, a presentation consultant and speaker in Minneapolis offers affirmations or compliments to people she just meets, to break the ice. "Sometimes I even do this before I say my name or ask for theirs," she says. "People love to get compliments and this can be a terrific conversation starter."

Ryan McCormick, President of Rising Sun PR on Long Island, New York, recalls one of the best introductory lines he ever received at a networking event: "It's one of those networking meetings where you have to wear clothes, huh?" Using humor in this way is a great way to connect with someone rapidly (but refrain of course, from anything that could be perceived as offensive). As for McCormick, he usually just says, "My name is Ryan," while offering a firm handshake, and that works well for him. Other equally simple, yet excellent conversation starters include:

- "What brings you here?"
- "Have you attended this event before?"
- "Do you know many people here?"
- "What type of business are you in?"
- "What made you come to this event?"

Ask Away

Keep in mind that seasoned networkers as well as newbies attend networking events. People who have been successfully networking for a long period of time can tell very quickly which newbie they will or will not want to network with. How? "If the person doesn't share an interest in getting to know me, and doesn't seem like a giver, then I do not want to connect with them," says Justin Krane, Certified Financial Planner at Krane Financial Solutions in Los Angeles. "I do not view myself as a taker, but don't want to network with people who aren't warm, inviting, and friendly."

Show that you are an affable giver by taking an interest in the person you have just met. One of the best techniques for doing so is by asking open-ended questions (as opposed to those that require a "Yes" or "No" response), which opens the door to follow-up conversation. But do remember that you are here for a specific purpose, and that is to help move someone else's business forward. So ask questions designed to offer you solid information that will help you help your new acquaintance.

Five Best Networking Questions

1. "What's the best part of your job?"
2. "How do you typically spend your day?"
3. "What's the most difficult aspect of your work?"
4. "Who can I introduce you to in this room?"
5. "How can I help you with your business?"

The last question is the most important of all, and always makes me smile when I ask this, because it generally triggers a surprised look by my new contact. Think about it: how often do you ask someone you know on a business level what you can do for him or her? But that is exactly what networking is about—doing for others. In the long run, you do often receive back what you give.

Dress for Success

Be sure you are ready to attend the event. This means you're wearing a jacket with pockets or pants/skirt with pockets. In your right pocket, you have business cards, so you can access them with ease. You should also have a pen to jot notes down on the back of the cards of the people you meet so when you follow up (which is critical), you can refer to what you wrote.

Working the Room

Be sure to position yourself at the entrance of the room as people are arriving. But once the gathering is in full swing, maneuver your way around the room by starting on the outside of the group along the wall and walk the wall, introducing yourself to every single person that you see.

An effective networker can work a room by moving around, but in all probability, most people in the room aren't moving, because they haven't figured out the host/hostess act yet. But you have, so once you've worked your way around the outside perimeter of the room, make your way into the center. Make eye contact, say hello, and shake hands warmly and firmly. Talk to each individual by asking what he or she does and why he or she is there. Once you know why these people are in attendance, it's easy to figure out to whom to introduce them. Keep each person you meet in mind as you work your way around the room, all the while considering who you can match up. Remember, you are all at the same dance, the same party—it's just that you know what to do! Keep connecting as you go along, but don't just point out Jim to Sue; take Sue over to meet Jim and introduce them. That is, after all, what a gracious host/hostess does.

Do ask for business cards, but don't give out your card unless someone directly asks for it. If they don't ask for your card (that's a clue that they aren't good networkers), ask if you may give them your card. Handing over a card before it's requested is not proper etiquette. I'm often baffled at networking events in which people are just running around giving out their cards. "What am I supposed to do with this? I know nothing about you," I say to myself. Chances are, I'm not the only one asking myself that same question, leaving those individuals randomly handing out their business cards actually in worse shape than before they entered the room.

You may be nervous and shy as you practice these networking skills, but do remember to smile throughout. If you appear grumpy or miserable, chances are, people will not want to connect with you. And although a smile won't guarantee a new contact or ensure a valuable new connection, it will go a long way in helping to strike up a conversation and being the person that people *want* to talk to at an event and, hopefully, do business with sometime in the future.

So while "starting the party" may not always be easy, it's one of the most important things that you can do as a networker. Once started, the party can move into full swing—conversations can turn into contacts, phone numbers can turn into future meetings, and a night of networking can turn into new business. But the first step, as with all good parties, is to get things off the ground. And that first step lies with *you*. So get your conversation starters ready.

As a Fast Track Networker, You Now Know:

- Think about networking events as parties, rather than business functions, and keep in mind that there are many strangers attending, not just you.

- Start conversations. Ask questions, and make sure they are open-ended to move the dialogue forward and keep it interesting.

- Work your way around the room, so you are able to meet as many people as possible. Offer a warm greeting, and a firm handshake.

- Networking is about connecting, not selling. Avoid selling at all costs, and avoid those who want to sell to you. Those are not people who want to network.

- Dress appropriately, have business cards on hand, but don't hand them out unless they are requested.

I can recall feeling a little queasy when I first began attending networking events. Entering a room where there are so many people talking to each other can be extremely intimidating. So, one of the ways I overcame this was by asking someone to attend events with me. Eventually, I became much more comfortable with the process, so my best advice is, don't give up, take a friend along and you'll get the hang of it.

—Bridget Doyle, pharmacist,
Discount Drug Mart
Westlake, Ohio

Chapter Three
No Time for Awkwardness

Navigating Around a Networking Function

Every social situation has potential for awkward moments. Who hasn't been at a party where a person you've just met is hogging all of your time and attention and you can't figure out how to make your getaway? What about the person who has one too many martinis and is now making a complete fool of himself in front of 100 people? How about the person you've been chatting with for a half hour, who can't remember your name, even though you said it several times? Networking events are no exception. In fact, for those who are not accustomed to these, making your way around an event with finesse can be challenging.

Suppose you're chatting it up with someone you've just met for the first time, and inside you know it's time to end the conversation and move on. Is it rude to excuse yourself? How do you do it gracefully? More important-ly, how do you do it without insulting your new contact, and leaving the door open for a future relationship with him/her, or perhaps one of *his or her* contacts? The last thing you want to do is potentially burn a bridge at a networking event, when the purpose of being there is to build as many new connections as possible.

Unlike a party, where it's fine to socialize with one or two people if you hit it off and are enjoying yourself, the purpose of networking events is to meet many individuals—ideally, everyone in the room. So concluding conversa-tions and moving on to meeting others is not rude; in fact, it's expected. In this chapter, you'll learn how to ex-tricate yourself effectively from someone who just won't let go and other potentially uncomfortable situations that might occur during an event.

Keep Conversations Brief

As self-appointed "host/hostess" of networking events, you recognize that in order to introduce yourself to everyone in the room and figure out how to meet their needs (meaning, either connect them to others on the spot or jot down notes for follow up later), you can't spend an hour with each guest. You can't even spend a half hour with each guest. Nor should you, even if you have hours to kill. Instead, make it a point to keep con-versations brief—up to 10 minutes tops—with every new connection. That's all you really need to ask the right questions about who they are, why there are attending the event, what they do, and, most importantly, how you can help them.

Let's say you've met someone who you have immediate synergy with. The more you talk, the more you both realize that you are a great business match. You want to converse with this person all night, trading business stories, talking about business trends and other mutual interests. Tempting, considering how easy it is to talk to this person, and how "safe" it is to not have to make the effort to move back into the networking pool and strike up yet another conversation. Don't do it. Exchange business cards; let the person know how happy you are that you've met, that you will be calling to set up a time to talk further during the week, and move on. Remember, you have scores of guests to greet. And while it may indeed be more difficult (and maybe not as much fun) to engage in other conversations, short conversations with as many people as you can will pay off in the long run.

Listen Attentively

With so many people to meet, and so little time, it's easy to become distracted when you are speaking to a new contact at a networking event. But if you are not fully hearing the person you're conversing with, you are wasting both your time and theirs. And if you think that the person you are talking to doesn't notice the way you are scanning the crowd for other potential people to speak with, or looking over his or her shoulder to see who may be entering the room, think again. People notice. Not only that, but they also probably won't think much of someone who doesn't seem to be giving their conversation the priority it warrants, and probably won't give your future follow-up call the priority *you'll* be looking for!

Mark Amtower, a partner at Amtower & Company in Highland, Maryland, has experienced this firsthand at networking events, but takes it in stride. "If they are not interested, I move on," he says. "It is not worth the effort to cultivate a forced relationship. There are always more people to meet. Don't take offense if someone does not pay attention—simply move on."

Remember, the point of attending networking functions is to connect with and help others. How can you do so, when you are not paying attention to what they are telling you about themselves? And responding to their questions with answers that show little or no thought ("Yeah, the food is good here") not only shows lack of interest, but may indicate that you just don't find them interesting enough to talk to, even if that's not the case.

One good way to stay focused is to maintain eye contact. In addition, once you've asked for the person's business card, jot down notes on the back of it that will remind you who this person is, and how you might help him or her at a later date. This will also show the person you're speaking to that you are engaged and interested in what he or she saying.

Lastly, good networkers will want to know about *you* during your 10-minute chat. Be prepared to tell them succinctly and enthusiastically by practicing your 30-second elevator pitch way before the event. An elevator pitch is a brief overview of what you do, condensed into a short, but comprehensive description that you could give during the span of an elevator ride to someone who asked about your business or what you do for a living. Be clear and precise about what you do—there just isn't enough time to be coy or funny here, or to have the person try to guess. And be prepared to answer questions about not only your job, but also your industry. Good networkers will be asking you all kinds of questions that will help them connect you to their best contacts.

Moving On

So you've spoken to a good number of people, you feel great and upbeat about the event so far, but all of a sudden you are in the throes of a "Debbie Downer" type of person. This is someone who can find a gloomy thing to say about every single topic of conversation. And I've come across many such types at networking events, unfortunately. This is especially true during times of economic instability. But I read the papers. I know what's going on. I don't want to hear it from someone I just met at a networking event. So if the person you are talking to is negative or a downer, change the subject. Spin the conversation about the terrible economy to opportunities in business. If the person continues to be a sourpuss, remember, you only have to chat with him for a few minutes before moving on to meet someone else!

Ending a conversation and moving on to another connection requires a bit of finesse. You don't want to seem rude. You don't want to leave your new contact standing there by himself/herself. And mostly, you don't want to leave the person you've been talking to with a negative "last impression" of you ditching him or her to try to find someone else to talk to. But there are certain "tricks" that will allow anyone to master the fine art of leaving a conversation, without leaving a negative impression on someone you just spent 10 minutes trying to impress.

Here's how I do it. As I see someone walking by, I discreetly turn and draw that person into my conversation by saying, "Hi, how are you?" Now the person has to stop and respond. Once that happens, I introduce myself and my new networking acquaintance. I spend a few more seconds with them, and then ease out of the conversation. Sometimes I will say something like, "I will leave the two of you to get to know each other" or I will say, "See you later; I'm off to find new people to introduce to the two of you!" This works well for me; not only am I removing myself from the exchange, but I'm also connecting others on the spot. Everyone's happy. I've helped others "break the ice" and potentially form a new relationship, and I've allowed myself to leave the conversation in a positive, upbeat way, rather than the standard, awkward conversation lull followed by an equally awkward, "It was nice meeting you."

Of course, businesspeople that are successful at networking have their own tried-and-true techniques. To extricate herself from conversations, Seattle freelance writer and editor Karin Carter says she uses "wrap-up language" such as, "It's been so nice to meet you! Thank you for telling me about what you do. I'm going to mingle a little/go say hello to Ann/step out for a moment…"

Jeff Goldberg, president of Jeff Goldberg & Associates, a sales training and consulting firm in New York, is direct, but tactful: "Well, there are a lot of people here and I don't want to hog all your time. It was great meeting you! Enjoy the rest of the event."

Florida Democratic County Chairs Association Chairwoman Alison Morano notes that a polite and direct method works best for her, as well. "I usually just mention that there are other people we should both be speaking with and that I'll see them soon," she states.

Social Blunders

Whereas nametags are an obvious way to remember people's names as you meet them (and although probably all of us hate wearing them, we do have to admit that they *do* come in handy), they are not always provided at networking functions. If a nametag is provided by the hosts, place it on the right side of your body, either on the lapel or adjacent to where the lapel would be so when you shake hands, the person's eyes focus to the right and align with the name tag. Recalling the names of new acquaintances is challenging for the majority of people, so don't feel inadequate if a contact's name goes in one ear and out the other, especially at networking events, where you are meeting many people for the first time.

In order to recall someone's name, "I repeat the person's name two times in my head and at least twice, preferably three times, in the conversation," says Joshua Christensen of Albuquerque, New Mexico. He also reads the business card as it's handed to him, so the name is repeated visually. Use whatever method works best for you, but if you forget the person's name, it's perfectly fine to say so with a simple, "I'm sorry, what is your name again?"

Wining and Dining

People always ask me how to handle food at these sort of events, because if you've been to a few you know first-hand that eating and networking don't always go hand-in-hand. You should eat something before you go to a networking dinner. This way, you aren't one of the people standing in a long buffet line, starving. Those people are most likely standing there and not only starving, but feeling put off that they are wasting their time standing in line. So, if you eat a little something before you go to a lunch or dinner event, you won't have a need to stand in line.

If you forget to eat before the event, and have a desperate need to grab a little something from the buffet, you should not network while you wait in line. You are limited to the guy in front of you and the gal in back of you, all lamenting about how the guy in the front of the line is hogging all the shrimp. Instead, use this time to visually seek out a good spot in the room so that when you do have your plate of food, you can inch your way over there and observe what's going on around you. Think of this as your time to take a needed break from all of the networking you have been doing all evening.

Finally, often you will come across alcohol at networking events, but in my experience it's best not to drink. Remember, while it looks and feels like a party, it's not. You are at a business function and want to be at the top of your game at all times. Take a pass on the alcohol and pass the time, instead, by engaging in some lively conversations that will translate into the new contacts that you're looking for. That is after all, the real reason that you're there. Many people believe that because alcohol is available, it's perfectly fine to partake. But I've seen a CEO dance on a table (which was the topic of conversation for months). I've heard the head of a very well-known organization give an incredibly drunken speech that left people in the audience with their mouths wide open. I've seen someone throw up on a table full of VIP's—and all of this because they drank alcohol. If there is the slightest hint that you can't just have one, then don't! Also, alcohol stinks badly! No one wants to talk in small groups smelling like a martini or a vat of wine. So if you encounter someone at an event who has had too much and he or she wants to talk to you, it's much better to gracefully find a way to get away. Nothing you say is going to leave any sort of impact on them anyway, so walk away, nicely.

When the Party's Over

As a novice networker, you may be asking, how do you know when it's time to leave the event? What if you haven't spoken to some people that you wanted to meet? Well, you only have a certain amount of time at these events, so make every minute count. Always bear in mind that you don't want to spend too much time with any one particular individual. But if you find yourself in a situation where you didn't have a chance to meet a few of the key people attending, don't worry. If people are leaving, you don't need to rush to meet them; that isn't the goal. You don't have to meet everyone in the room, especially if by the end of the evening you've made some good contacts to follow up with. This wasn't a one-shot thing. This is the first of many events you will be attending and chances are, you are going to see those people again. If it's imperative that you connect right away, give the person a call the following day. Say something like, "I was hoping we'd get a chance to meet last night, but I didn't have an opportunity to say hello. I'm so and so...."

Lastly, you know it's time for *you* to leave the event when you feel as though you've accomplished what you came to the event for (or when you start to notice the room thinning out). If there were a couple of people in particular that you met that you said you would follow up with and they are still there, say goodbye, and that you will call within the next of couple days to get together is a very nice parting remark. If the event host is visible, thanking him or her for putting on the event is also appropriate.

When you have attended an event that was successful for you, you know it. You know by how you feel, the types of conversations you had, the people you connected with, and the people you connected others with at the event—not by the number of business cards in your pocket! If you only talked to two people and they were people you already knew, you probably aren't going to feel as good as if you met four new people, and introduced those four people to the two people you already knew.

Smooth Sailing

When done right, sailing through a networking event may seem effortless to those watching on the sidelines. But the truth is people who appear to be seamlessly and smoothly "working the room" actually have put a lot of work into their approach and networking style. So the next time you witness some fabulous networkers, know that there was some real preparation and practice behind their performances. And afterward, they put in an equal amount of work. Going to a networking event is a great way to meet people, but that's only part of the story. The real key to successful networking lies in the follow-up.

You have 48 hours for an effective follow-up, and e-mail isn't the way to do it. If you met 30 people and 10 of them are people you want to develop relationships with, either because you can do something for them or because you believe they may be a benefit to you and others you know, call them. Invite them for coffee, invite them for a "get to know you better lunch," invite them to meet for a half hour. And when you do meet, don't sell them. You have invited them to meet because you want to get to know them better. Bring something of interest when you meet—an article about their business, a couple of names and numbers of people you know that you think they would enjoy meeting. Remember, you are together to start a wonderful networking relationship.

Think about it. Walking into a room full of people you may not know, and people who you want to do business with but may not have had the chance to meet until now, may seem awkward, but everyone in the room is there for the same reason. So lose the awkwardness, take your strategic position in the room, and navigate the crowd using the secrets of today's most successful networkers.

As a Fast Track Networker, You Now Know:

- Before attending any networking event, perfect your 30-second elevator pitch and practice it out loud so it becomes second nature. You don't want to seem hesitant, unsure of yourself/your business or, worse yet, fumble with words when someone meets you for the first time.

- You are there to meet and connect with many people in one evening. In order to do so, don't spend more than 10 minutes with anyone.

- Don't allow yourself to get stuck with someone who is a downer. Instead, change whatever he or she says to an upbeat comment. Avoid someone who's a hanger-on—a person who just wants to spend time with you, and keeps you away from connecting with others. The best way to disengage is to pull someone else into the conversation you are having, introduce the two people, and move on.

- Networking events are not a place to have long, involved conversations about your personal life or your business. They're also not a place to make a sale. You are there to meet new people and to connect them with others in your circle.

- The best way to make a networking function work for you is by hearing what others are saying, so do less talking and more listening.

- Avoid eating at these events, if you can. Otherwise, you may waste a lot of time standing in a long buffet line when you can be networking instead. And even if you find that having one alcoholic beverage relaxes you, don't drink at networking events. You are there to do business, even if the ambiance is party-like.

- Following up is key to networking. Without follow-up, there is no point in taking time out of your schedule to attend networking functions.

And when following up, never sell. Instead, invite the person for coffee, lunch, or a quick meeting in his or her office. Bring something of value, such as a newspaper article, that the person you are meeting will enjoy reading. This shows that you are a person who has his or her best interests at heart and who wants to help with his or her business. It shows that you are the kind of person who commits and who is reliable and trustworthy—someone everyone will want to network with.

It happens at every networking situation I'm in: I meet someone I want to talk to the entire time! But I understand that I am there to meet many people, and also, I would never want to monopolize all of someone else's time.
—Emily Leach, CEO of SEO Strategy Group
Serving the World on the World Wide Web

FASTTRACKNETWORKINGFASTTRACKN
KNETWORKINGFASTTRACKNETWORKIN
KINGFASTRACKNETWORKINGFASTTRAC
RACKNETWORKINGFASTTRACKNETWOR
ORKINGFASTTRACKNETWORKINGFAST
ASTTRACKNETWORKINGFASTTRACKNET
ETWORKINGFASTTRACKNETWORKINGF
GFASTTRACKNETWORKINGFASTTRACK

Chapter Four
Small Group, Big Results

Mastering the art of networking means more than learning how to navigate large crowds and work the room at big networking functions. In fact, some of the biggest networking success stories across the board come from what I like to call "intimate networking"—small scale events in intimate, personal, and often one-on-one settings. These can run the gamut from breakfast networking meetings at a local diner to a casual lunch with colleagues and/or friends, to after-work get-togethers at places where professionals in your area tend to gather.

If you have a difficult time in large crowds, places where you don't really have the opportunity to talk to someone for an extended period of time, especially if you want to make your way around the room, these smaller gatherings, or "intimate networking" opportunities, may be a better fit for you. Personally, while I know attending large networking functions is a crucial part of networking and something that I must do, I would rather sit down with eight or so people and have direct conversations about business and how we can help each other. It's more relaxed. It's more productive. And for me, it's just more fun!

My networking friend Donna Drake, president of Drake Media in Plainview, New York, agrees. "Generally those of us that are the most outgoing and overtly friendly are the ones that networking comes to naturally, both in larger group settings and in smaller settings. However, I have found over the years that when I have had the opportunity to network in a very small setting, that the synergy formed and the outcome of that synergy tends to skew to a higher intensity and an overall more successful outcome." Through her smaller networking group, Donna was able to connect with people who helped her launch her TV show, "Live It Up with Donna Drake and Fran Capo." She'd been seeking production people, but it wasn't until she discussed it with a fellow networker in her smaller group that the ball got rolling. That intimate setting enabled her to communicate exactly what she required. One contact led to another and today, her show is fully staffed with people that came highly recommended to her.

First Impressions

Small groups, where there are few distractions, offer great opportunities to make meaningful connections. In fact, it's here where you will be remembered by how you introduce yourself to the group and by your appearance and overall demeanor. Making an excellent first impression is not only important, it's critical. And just as the saying goes, not only do you "never get a second chance to make a first impression," but when it comes to networking, if you blow your first impression, you may never get a chance to have a second meeting.

I have observed closely what people respond to and what they don't in terms of introductions from guests that attend the meetings. I often wonder if the people who have made a terrible first impression ever wonder why they aren't invited back. The worst offenders are those that think that they are there to tell us their whole life story, usually in a very depressing "woe is me" fashion—"Business is bad, and that's why I'm here." "The economy is horrible, that's why I'm here." "I don't get any referrals, that's why I'm here." "My husband/wife/cousin/whatever works with me and is draining the business, that's why I'm here." I've heard it all, and these people look to the group to save them. They go on and on and are so self-absorbed with their issues, that they aren't even aware of the fact that our eyes are glazing over and that they are annoying, depressing, and not giving at all. No one is going to want to do business with negative people. Who wants to be around them? Networking groups don't exist to save anyone.

In addition to those who just want to share their sob stories, I've seen many others make a bad first impression in other ways. For instance, there are people who just talk too much in general. They take too long to introduce themselves, and they give too many details about their business: they talk about their clients, they talk about their employees, they talk about what they want and need endlessly. They don't mention who they know, what they have to give, or that they understand the principles of a mutually beneficial working relationship. Then there are those who interrupt and are disruptive during a meeting. They check their PDA, they interrupt the people speaking, they ask questions at inappropriate times. In short, they need to be center stage at all times. There are people who say things that are completely wrong for a business function, such as tell a sexist joke or make some kind of political statement.

Then there are the group "hoppers." These are people who just attend group meetings, never joining, never getting involved, never really being there, yet they show up everywhere. They go to all the meetings and they attend all the groups, at least once, and they are there to take. They do their introduction, then they spend 10 minutes handing out their literature, their cards, brochures, coupons for discounts, whatever they have with them—and you never see them again. But you do hear about them. In a business community, their names will surface time and time again, and so will their poor reputations. When it comes to small scale groups and meetings, every person who makes an impression one way or another, will be remembered.

All Eyes on You

Being memorable, of course, is the goal (you want others to keep you in mind, so when something comes up that might be beneficial for you, they contact you. And you can be assured that in an intimate networking setting, all eyes and ears are going to be on you when it's your turn to introduce yourself to the group. There will be no distractions of hors doeuvres being passed around, or the low din of background conversations, so perfect your introduction and positive attitude in advance. This will ensure that you are self-confident and that you are someone people not only want to connect with, but want to get to know further. "I mentally put all my work issues 'on the shelf' and prepare to be in the moment and meet new, exciting people," says Dawn Veselka, president of Out of the Blue Delivered, in Oviedo, Florida. "I go with the principle that you can learn something new from everyone you meet, so I get excited to meet new people."

Before attending a networking meeting, "I remind myself that I am confident, happy, and open to meeting new people," says Christina L. Pollack, president of the Monterey County Young Professionals Group. "I've found that smiling and being friendly encourages communication amongst strangers. Also, wear a bright colored top. Whenever I wear yellow or orange, I find that people are the most drawn to or comfortable chatting with me. Color has a psychological effect on people."

Wisely Wait

Although it's always a good idea to take the lead at networking events (it shows that you are a go-getter and take-charge type of person), in small scenarios, you don't want to be the first person to speak. That's because first, you want to get a feel for the energy in the room, see how others present themselves, and watch the body language of the others in attendance. This is a strategy that works for Sudhir Sachdev, president of New York City-based Imaginewaves, Inc. "Frequently, I have seen that many people meet each other in networking events, push business cards, or otherwise draw attention to themselves without analyzing their surroundings. For myself, I let myself hang back and wait for the right or almost natural time to involve myself in a discussion before I will go forward with my information."

But what if it's up to the group leader as to who speaks first, and he picks you? That's okay! You will be ready with your introduction, regardless. Don't stumble and don't say, "I didn't want to go first, I don't know what to say." Don't make excuses. Of course you know what to say, you are introducing yourself! "My name is so and so." You know what you do for a living, so say that, too. "I am a relationship banker with Anderson Savings and Loan." You know what your position is and what you do all day, so add that. "My job is to meet as many people in the business community here in Henderson, and to help them build their businesses through loan assistance, credit counseling, and introductions to each other as business people whenever I can see a match between two people." Then follow up with the most important thing in the end—what you can do for the other people. You could have easily said, "My job is to meet as many business people as I can in Henderson so I can add you to our e-mail list, flood your mailbox with offerings from our bank, hound you until you open a business checking account with us, and call on you in hopes that you will introduce me to your friends, coworkers, family, and other businesses you know. Now, if you could all pass your business cards to me, I will be in touch."

Guess which introduction will guarantee positive responses? Keep your introduction short. Keep it simple and speak up. Don't stumble and be sure to smile throughout.

Now if you don't have to go first, you are in a great position to sit back and listen/watch and observe closely how others introduce themselves. Watch for body language of the guests who are listening. Are they fidgeting because the person is too long-winded? Are they writing things down because the person talking is a person with great contacts and they don't want to miss anything? Are they talking to their neighbors? Remember, building a networking relationship, or any kind of relationship for that matter, is about trust. Can you be trusted to be aware of your surroundings and not take center stage? Can you be trusted enough to be friendly and not hurtful or backstabbing? Can you be trusted enough to be giving? You really can learn a lot from watching others in this type of small gathering, so be aware of how you feel when someone is talking. See if the person seems approachable, self-absorbed, or doesn't stop handing out business cards when another person is speaking.

Speaking of pushing business cards—don't do it. Inevitably, the first or second person to introduce him- or herself during an intimate function will pull out business cards and, probably rather awkwardly, start passing them around the table while speaking. This is exactly what you should not do, so at all costs, resist the temptation to follow suit. Why? Because I can bet that the others at the table are finding it intrusive and distracting. In this kind of intimate scenario, the idea is to make face-to-face contact and to listen to each other attentively. When a business card is being passed around a table as someone is speaking to a group, it invites individuals to focus on the item being routed around the room from one person to another, then to focus their eyes on the card itself. Listening to the speaker then takes a backseat to the action around the table.

Speaking Out

All eyes will be on you when it's your turn to speak. Again, begin with your name, then your company name, followed by a two-sentence (at the most) description of what you do. Be sincere. Be yourself. Be genuine. In my opinion, it's best to stick with straightforward information about your position and company. Some networking groups encourage cute introductions, which require group members to spend hours figuring out how to say they sell insurance, or that they own a restaurant, and so they say things like "I protect families" or "I provide sustenance when there isn't anything to eat at home." But all you need to say is, "I sell insurance" or "I own a restaurant." Don't make others have to guess what you do. You aren't going to be memorable by making something sound cute and clever. What they'll remember is someone who perhaps tried a bit too hard instead of being straightforward. And they'll probably remember that they didn't like it.

The final thing you should say after introducing yourself, your business, and offering to share your connections with the group, is thank you to the host who invited you to the event, and a statement such as, "I look forward to meeting each of you one-on-one so I can be aware of who you want to meet and what your business focus is, so I can help you better." There isn't anything clever involved. It's a straight-up, from the heart, this is who I am, this is what I do, and this is what I can do for you statement. Now *that's* memorable!

Your Business Card

When it comes to the expected business card exchange, timing is everything. Wait until after all attendees are finished introducing themselves and wait for the host to invite you to pass your business cards around to the group. If the host doesn't do this (some don't and some may just forget), wait until after the meeting and walk up to every individual, shake hands, tell each of them it was a pleasure to meet them, and ask them for their card. Although it may go against your gut feeling, do *not* offer your card unless they ask for it. If they don't ask for yours, don't give them one. This is just common business etiquette that unfortunately, many people don't follow. My guess is it's because they don't know the protocol and simply assume that handing out business cards at any random opportunity is appropriate. Keep the cards in your pocket unless asked, and you just may keep the door open for a future contact.

What to Bring

In addition to business cards to hand out on request, I often bring with me a one- or two-page referral "cheat sheet" about my business. Peter Reiss, president of Feng Shui by Peter Reiss in Northport, New York, shared with me this idea and it's been one of the most copied things in networking circles I have ever seen. It's easier for people to refer businesses to you if they really know what you do, so make it very simple and clear for them.

Referral Cheat Sheet

smart|marketing
solutions group, inc.

SmartMarketing Solutions Group, Inc. is a marketing, public relations, graphic design and business development agency specializing in growing your business and increasing your bottom line.

Whether a company is looking for general marketing help, a complete branding campaign or to see your business or organization featured in key media outlets, we offer a wide range of services to provide your company with exactly what you need to get the results you want.

Our Services Include:

- Branding
- Business Image Enhancement
- Brochures/Newsletters
- Website Development
- Media Press Kits
- Community Awareness Campaigns
- Public Relations Campaigns
- Networking And Business Building
- Strategic And Creative Marketing Plans

- Business Development Programs
- Event Planning And Implementation
- Advertising
- Speakers Training
- Network & Business Building
- Event Concepts & Implementations
- Corporate Identity Programs
- Consulting

We serve:

- Small to medium size businesses
- Not for profit organizations
- Entrepreneurs, just starting out
- Entrepreneurs, growing, but want to grow faster
- Established Businesses That Are Looking To Reinvent Themselves

In the following industries:

- Business to Business
- Corporate & Professional Services
- Healthcare
- Hospitality and Food Service
- Fashion and Lifestyle
- Not for Profits
- And More!

2800 Utah NE
Albuquerque, NM 87110
P: 505.293.3553
F: 505.332.9375

695 Plainview Road
Bethpage, NY 11714
P: 516.222.0236
F: 516.222.2235

smart marketing, public relations,
graphic design and business development
for smart companies

REFERRAL CHEAT SHEET

DiBella
IRONWORKS

Since 1968, DiBella has been providing Long Island homes and businesses with the high quality, custom ironwork that not only adds an unsurpassed level of security – but adds a unique element of style, as well. With our iron window grills, doors, gates and railings, we've been "keeping Albuquerque safe" for decades – and remain the region's most established -- and respected -- ironworks business.

Our Services Include:

- Security Storm Doors
- Security Screen Doors
- Security Window Grills
- Ornamental Gates & Rails
- Window Film Technology -- Innovative Invisible Security & an Option to Traditional Security Bars
- Elegant and beautiful custom designed ironwork -- and a stunning addition to your home or business
- Electric or solar powered gates
- Offering a variety of state-of-the-art high-tech options, including entry cards, remote entries and keypads for gates
- Responsive, personalized service and repairs
- Evening & Saturday Estimates & Installations
- Emergency service is our specialty - immediate installations for immediate peace of mind
- All products come with a lifetime guarantee against defective workmanship and materials on the master frame for as long as you own your home

We serve:

- Residential
- Gated Communities
- Apartments
- Industrial

3109 Plainview Road, Bellmore, NY   PHONE: 516-345-1878   FAX: 516-345-1401   www.dibella.com

Referral Cheat Sheet

Doyle Health & Wellness Center

Doyle Health & Wellness Center have been launched in dozens of cities nationwide, and the Creating Wellness program is considered one of the most highly advanced wellness systems ever developed. Incorporated within the state-of-the-art Atchley Family Chiropractic practice, the new Doyle Health & Wellness Center in Cleveland will offer patients a complete health assessment and evaluation, followed by a customized wellness program that includes exercise, nutrition, personal development, stress management and education. Most importantly, the unique Creating Wellness System provides ongoing weekly consultations for each client with Dr. Matthew Doyle, a leader in health and wellness, and Dr. David Doyle, who founded Doyle Health & Wellness Center in 1967 and who has treated thousands of patients throughout the area.

Our Services Include:

- Wellness Assesments
- Creating Wellness System
- Customized Wellness Programs
- Adjustments
- Manipulations
- Weight Loss
- Custom Foot Orthotics

- X-Ray / MRI / CAT SCAN
- Ultrasound
- Electrical Muscle Stimulation
- Cryotherapy
- Interferential Stimulation
- Microcurrent Therapy
- SpineMED Decompression

We serve people who would like to:

- Get healthy
- Maintain health
- Turn fatigue to energy
- Regain strength
- Achieve a restful night of sleep
- Get rid of pain forever

- Lose weight
- Improve the work life balance between career and family
- Looking for nutritional counseling
- Help their family reach optimal levels of wellbeing

Be Fit. Eat Right. Think Well.

3150 Holly Drive, Cleveland, OH 44222 • 216-265-5651 • www.Doyle Health & Wellness Center.com

Referral Cheat Sheet

Feng Shui
by Peter Reiss

Feng Shui by Peter Reiss is a specialized consultancy focused on bringing the joy and passion of LOVE into people's lives through guided adjustments to their home environment.

Love energy helps bring abundance into all areas of life including wealth, health, family and friends.

Our Services Include:

Individual consultations for:
- Singles seeking love
- Couples who want to strengthen their love
- Life issues

Speaking and teaching:
- Seminars
- Lunch and Learns
- Workshops
- Keynotes

Our Ideal Client:

Single, widowed or divorced women or gay men between the age of 35 and 55, earning a comfortable living in the six figure range, who are looking to find a love relationship. They may have been in the "dating scene" for a while without great success and are frustrated with the process.

They also may be in a new relationship and are looking to deepen it into love and, perhaps, into a permanent commitment.

They may belong to organizations such as Parents Without Partners or attend many single functions like speed-dating, all without great success. (Those organizations are ideal for our presentations.)

Most importantly – they've been "looking for love in all the wrong places" and really, really want that to change!

www.fengshuiconsults.com • info@FengShuiConsults.com

Ensuring Contact With Everyone

I can't reiterate enough how essential it is to end the meeting by moving about the room and shaking the hand of every person in attendance. Adding this personal touch, making eye contact and offering a firm handshake, or perhaps noting something memorable that they've said or something that you have in common is exactly the point of intimate networking meetings. And not only are you showing that you are a serious professional, but you are also showing you are highly attentive by making each person you meet feel important. Everyone likes to feel important and valued, especially when they are putting themselves out there on the line at any type of a networking function, whether a large gathering or intimate setting. After all, don't you feel significant when someone takes the time out to reach out to you specifically at a gathering?

Be sure to leave a tip for the server, even if you've paid for your beverage or meal in advance. Leave a dollar or two and people will notice that you are a giver of all sorts.

Do Your Own Thing

There are all sorts of out-of-the-box places to engage in intimate networking, such as golf outings. I once had an employee who was a great golfer, and I don't mean she was great in terms of how she played, but she knew the rules, she understood golf etiquette, and most importantly, she knew how to network. I would send her to play in all the golf outings we could afford, making sure they were outings where there were people we wanted to connect with. I would send her on her own, but we would call the organizer, find out who was playing, and then ask if she could play with this person or these three people. I can't tell you how much business she got from this form of intimate networking. And that includes one of our largest, on-going clients in the real estate industry. She landed him on the back nine of a golf outing and I can assure you, that was the best $500 I have ever spent!

Lastly, if you have trouble finding an outlet for some productive "intimate networking" or can't seem to find the right small group to meet your networking needs, start your own. Even if the group is small, the long-term pay-off will be big. Consider these two examples:

Freelance writer Iyna Bort Caruso, who runs Sweet Lime Ink in Rockville Centre, New York, found that while general business networking groups were beneficial to growing her business, a lot of her work came from referrals and leads from other writers. That's when she decided to form her own small networking group of professional freelancers, many of whom she'd known only online through social media connections. "The monthly face-to-face meetings provide a framework for support, trust, and camaraderie among members," she says. The group exchanges information about media outlets they wish to work with, keeps up on editorial changes at various publications, encourages each other to pursue their writing goals, and shares valuable sources. "Through group leads, I wound up teaching a workshop, acquired a new client, and got a great referral for technical support services that saved me time and money."

Jeff Weiner, president of HKM Associates, a Long Island, New York, insurance brokerage firm, is one professional who not only recognized the value of intimate networking, but did something about it. Jeff started the Roundtable Networking Group, which is one of the coolest networking ideas I've heard of and one of the best networking scenarios I've ever experienced. Twice a week, he invites 12 people that he thinks should know each other to a local restaurant. Those who are invited never know in advance who else will be attending, but Jeff is very thoughtful about putting each particular group of people together. Each attendant pays for his/her own meal, and the conversation is stimulating and thoughtful. I'm not quite sure how he manages to pull it off, but there is always synergy between the guests. It's a lot of work for Jeff, but the return has been enormous. Everyone wants to be invited. It's incredibly cool (and a "badge of honor") to be one of Jeff's guests. People talk about who was there, and who may be invited to the following meeting. By thinking out-of-the-box and consistently providing local business people with an intimate forum to get to know each other, Jeff has become the "go to guy" for the hottest intimate networking on Long Island.

As a Fast Track Networker, You Now Know:

- Intimate networking works and sometimes, it can work better for certain individuals than networking in larger settings. But to be an intimate networker, the first step is finding (or creating) some unique intimate network settings that *you* can be part of.

- There are no second chances when it comes to first impressions, so make sure you are confident and self-assured. Do pay attention to how others behave at these meetings. Listen to your gut feeling about people you are meeting for the first time. If these are people who are not making a good impression upon you, steer clear of networking with them. If they are not making a good impression on you, chances are, they will never make a good impression on your contacts.

- Being the first one to speak isn't necessary; in fact, it's discouraged. Get a feel for the room and the people in the room first. But if you are called upon to be first, don't shy away. Be confident that what you have to say is important to everyone in attendance.

- Speaking clearly and succinctly when introducing yourself will make a good impact on everyone present. Do not give out your business cards while introducing yourself. And always thank the host for putting the meeting together.

- Never give out your business card, unless it's directly requested, but do go around the room and say goodbye to everyone in attendance. Let them know it was great meeting them and that you look forward to future contact.

- A "cheat sheet" stating what you do is a great way to communicate with people you've just met, if the conversation turns to, "Do you have any information you could leave with me?"

- Consider non-traditional intimate networking possibilities, such as golf outings. And if you can't seem to find a good intimate networking venue for your specific needs, start one of your own. You'll be pleasantly surprised by the rewards, and all the hard work that you put into starting your own group will be priceless.

I enjoy attending all kinds of networking meetings, but I have to admit, the early morning breakfast networking groups that I've belonged to have been extremely beneficial to me. There's just a different kind of energy at small meetings and I've made not only incredible business connections, but also good friends at these meetings.

—Christine McFarland,
director of Sales and Marketing,
ServPro of Parma/Seven Hills
Parma, Ohio

Chapter Five

If You Create It, They Will Come

With so many existing networking events and groups, it's likely that you've explored the wide variety of options out there as you work to find the right group (or groups) that best meets your needs. However, in addition to continuing to actively participate in the events and meetings that seem like a good fit for you, you may want to consider another route taken by many of the country's most notable networkers: starting your own networking group. As you saw in the previous chapter, this can often serve your specific industry needs, or match your personality.

As an entrepreneur and a leader, I am always looking for ways to do things better and differently, and I'm not happy unless I'm leading the pack. I'm not a follower, and that was probably one of the elements that prompted me to start my own networking group, Women on the Fast Track. Another was that there wasn't anything like it in the late 1980s. There were association meetings and there were some women's groups, but they didn't exist for the sole purpose of networking and business building. They were meetings that offered lunch or dinner and a speaker, and they weren't necessarily focused on networking. The meetings I was attending at the time were hit or miss, meaning you never really knew who would be there or if you would connect with anyone because these events weren't specifically designed for that. My group, WotFT, which has since grown from one chapter to many, was designed with relationships in mind. It was designed for small groups of women in business, or women responsible for bringing business to their companies and for the purpose of networking. No groups were (are) larger than 12 members and they meet every month at the same time, at the same place, and with the same goal—to help each other move their businesses forward. There is no other agenda. We don't have dinner, we don't have a speaker, and we don't do anything other than network.

Starting my own group was a daunting task. If you take on such an effort, it will take time and it will put your true entrepreneurial and networking skills to the test. It may be a while before it truly takes off, but it has brought me more valuable contacts, new business, and overall career success than I ever could have imagined.

Getting Started

Once you have made the decision to form your own networking group, the first step is to come up with a clever, memorable, and forward-thinking name for the group—one that will make everyone want to join. To this day, women who join my networking group comment that they love being part of an organization with such a powerful name, and one whose name really says it all in terms of where they are and where they want to be. Then decide if you want to keep it category-exclusive. For example, do you want only one banker, one insurance broker, one marketing professional, etc.? I suggest this approach, so there is no competition among members. However, you really need to consider this carefully. You may allow two people in the same industry, but serving distinct markets. For example, you may allow two public relations agencies who serve completely different clientele. One firm might handle consumer products exclusively. The other might deal only with high-tech clients. The same goes for law firms—one might specialize in matrimony and divorce, while the other only handles corporate accounts. Two retailers could also work together to network if one sells office furniture and the other sells maternity clothes. Chances are, there will never be competition between any of these while networking, but the networking opportunities would be plentiful.

Charging a Fee

Next, decide if you will be charging a membership fee. If you are uncertain about this, I highly recommend a fee. If you don't charge for membership, the perceived value of your group is diminished. And if there is no fee attached, people find it easier to not show up at the drop of a hat and/or to not take it seriously. I deliberately chose to make the fee for Women on the Fast Track somewhat high; it costs $500 for a one-year membership and oftentimes women will ask, "What do I get for that?" My response is usually something like this: "If you can't make back $500 from being in a networking group, you probably shouldn't join *any* networking group." The premise is, the more you pay, the more you will play.

Keep this in mind though: If you start your own group and charge fees, you are in fact starting a business and need to treat it as such. You need to determine what type of business it will be—sole proprietorship, corporation—and you need to register the business name with your state and open a checking account specific to the business, keep a separate set of books, and run your group like a second business. If you aren't going to charge fees, and just exist as a loosely based group that you've started, you don't have to do anything.

Ask yourself these questions:

- Do you have the time to run a second business?
- Do you have the motivation and staff to help you?
- Are you organized enough to take on this new endeavor?
- What are your long-term goals for this effort?
- How will this affect your income and taxes?
- How much time will you devote to this new venture each day?

If you accept money from members, you will be responsible for giving them their money's worth; not personally, but through your networking group's commitment. It will be up to you to keep the group motivated and energized.

And here's the good news: You can use the money you collect from membership dues to grow this new venture in a variety of ways. You can build a Website for your group, or a blog. You can use the money to place ads in local newspapers announcing your group and your group's activities. You can hold special events and use the money for special entertainment. You can (and should) print out collateral materials or premium items that you can give out to members and others. There are many things you can do with the collected funds to promote your new networking group, and to perhaps promote individual members. It's entirely up to you, because this is your business.

Finding a Place, Time, and Date

Your initial goal for your first meeting should be to have 10 to 15 people in attendance, so seek out small-scale locations such as local libraries, conference rooms within banks, law offices, and accounting offices. It's important that attendees have a comfortable, yet professional, environment that encourages conversation with the right seating configurations that will allow for both group discussions and hopefully some after-meeting mingling. Of course, finding a location that will allow you to continue to meet on a monthly basis at no charge is the goal, so look for any and all opportunities that may exist in your area and explore all existing contacts for any connections that they may have for possible meeting places. You never know just who might have access to their firm's conference room, or who may have a relative who owns a great restaurant with a small meeting room.

Once you've got a great name and the right location, you need to make sure to select an appropriate date and time for meetings. In fact, this can often be one of your most important decisions. You need to take into consideration the schedules of your potential members, and make it as convenient as possible for them to not only *want* to come, but to actually be able to be there on a regular basis without having to juggle the rest of their business and personal commitments. I know many networking groups who have breakfast meetings, way before the workday begins. But I have found that evening meetings—held from 6:00 p.m. to 7:30 p.m. work well. This way, people can either stay at work late and go directly to the meeting, or they have time to get home from work for a bit and then head back out. Of course, do your research ahead of time and try not to compete in terms of day/time with other networking groups—and make sure to pick a date at least two months ahead. You'll need at least that much time to develop an invitation and press release, as well as to distribute both to potential members and to the press to get the word out about the meeting.

Spreading the Word

You can have the coolest networking group name, the hottest location for your first meeting, and a date that's just right, but you may get a lukewarm reception to your new networking group if you neglect one critical factor: getting the word out about the group to others throughout the community. A simple press release providing all of the details of the meeting can and should be written and distributed to your local newspapers and magazines well in advance of the dates (most newspaper business calendar listings have a lead time of at least a few weeks and magazines are even longer). When writing your press release, be sure to include your contact information (including cell phone numbers), a brief introduction to your new networking group, plus the date, time, and location of your first meeting. In addition, include fee information for the initial meeting, if you are charging a fee to attend. Keep in mind that although I recommend charging a fee for group membership, the first meeting ought to be free. You want people to check it out, right? Also, "Free" is always a good selling point in a press release, and although the initial meeting should be free, the yearly membership fee is something that doesn't need to be highlighted in the meeting press release and is something that will be discussed at the meeting itself. Be sure to include a phone number for readers who wish to attend/RSVP. On page 96 is a sample press release that I've used for Women on the Fast Track. If this seems like something you may not be able to do, ask anyone you know who works for a public relations firm to write it for you. And perhaps you can offer that person a membership discount to your new networking group in exchange.

Women
on the Fast Track
An unbelievably fabulous networking organization
for business and professional women.

For Immediate Release
Contact: Lucy Rosen
516-222-0236 x123
Cell: 526-410-0423

WOMEN ON THE FAST TRACK HOLDS SEPTEMBER INTRODUCTORY NASSAU COUNTY CHAPTER 3 MEETING

Garden City, NY, August 2009 - On September 21, 2009 at 6 pm, Women on The Fast Track, (WOTFT), a national organization for business and professional women, will hold an introductory meeting in Woodbury, NY. The meeting will not only be an introduction to the organization, but will also offer women the opportunity to network.

WOTFT is a unique networking group for business and professional women that was launched in Nassau and Suffolk County in the later part of 2006. Comprised of smart, talented, successful, enterprising women willing to share information, contacts, resources, inspiration and their boundless energy, WOTFT has quickly grown to be one of the areas pre-eminent networking groups. The organization also has chapters in New Jersey and New Mexico.

The meeting will begin at 6 pm at Innovative Planning Services located at 80 Crossways Park West, Woodbury, NY and is open to all women professionals and business owners. For more
information about Women on the Fast Track, or how to become a member, please call Mary at 516-222-0236, visit www.womenonthefasttrack.com or email events@businessdevelopmentgroup.com.

###

Your Guest List

So how do you identify who to invite into your new networking group? Hopefully, if you are starting a group, you're starting it because you already have recognized in your mind a great group of people that would network well together. For example, are you in the catering business? You could easily invite into your new group all sorts of businesses that eventually might need catering services. However, why not identify a specific group of people such as wedding planners, florists, travel agents, bakers, transportation services, and photographers? All of these are in the wedding business, so networking amongst each other makes perfect sense.

However, here's a word of caution on who *not* to invite: people that don't know a lot of other businessmen and women. Starting a group is for those who are already out there, network well, know the game, even know how to potentially run a group (which takes some skill), and can easily put a group together. So the invitations should go to the specific people you want in your group and you should control who else is invited. Let's say you invite Mary, who is a travel agent, to attend your introductory meeting. Mary wants to attend, but she asks if she can bring a friend. It's perfectly within your rights to ask numerous questions about her companion, starting with what industry the friend is in (and if she has networked previously). If Mary's friend is also a travel agent, you may discourage her attendance, because since you want to keep your group category exclusive, Mary and her friend would be competing with each other if they both ended up joining the group.

Invitations should be concise, to the point, and explain exactly who you are, when and where you are meeting, and why. Here's a sample from my own group, Women on the Fast Track.

Where Can You Find a Network of Women...
Willing to share their resources, contacts, information and ideas?

Committed to helping you build your business?

Who realize that networking is essential for success?
Right Here.

Women
on the Fast Track

Please join us for our Nassau County Chapter 3 Launch

on Monday, January 18, 2010 from 6pm to 7:30pm
at Innovative Planning Services
located at 80 Crossways Park West, Woodbury, NY

WOTFT is a networking group that offers smart, talented, successful women the opportunity to establish strategic alliances with like-minded women. The group is comprised of those willing to share ideas, suggestions and resources to achieve professional and personal success. With several chapters in New Mexico, as well as New Jersey and New York, WOTFT has quickly grown to be one of the most pre-eminent networking organizations.

The introductory meeting is open to all
women professionals and business owners.

For more information about Women on the Fast Track,
please visit www.womenonthefasttrack.com.

To RSVP for the January meeting, please call 516-222-0236
or email events@businessdevelopmentgroup.com.
(You MUST RSVP to attend)

Introductory Meeting

For the introductory networking meeting, make sure you have on hand name tags, pens, a brochure or sheet explaining your goals for the networking group, a calendar listing of future meetings with the location and time for each, membership applications, a basket for business cards and, if you'd like, some snacks or beverages. The latter is not necessary, but it is a nice touch and certain to be appreciated by attendees.

Welcome everyone to the meeting and introduce yourself. It will be tempting to make your introductory speech all about what you do for a living, but do keep it brief and don't dwell on that. Remember that networking is all about helping others, so be sure to state who you know and what you can do for others in the group. Let everyone know, for example, that as an insurance broker, you have direct access to more than 5,000 business people who need professional services on a regular basis. Let them know what boards you sit on, what non-profits or foundations you are part of, and any other organizations you belong to that participants might be able to connect with.

Then go around the room and have everyone introduce themselves. They will probably fall into the trap of talking about what they do—the exercise is to find out what they can do to help others, so it will be up to you to gently steer them back to that intention. Once everyone is introduced, ask the group if they want to talk about what they are looking for by attending this networking group. There is one rule: No one can say they are looking for new business. That's a given. Instead, encourage them to be very precise. For example: "I'm looking for an introduction to the Vice President of Procurement at the NY State Department of Transportation." That's clear and direct. The more direct they are, the more specific they are, the better chance they will have to get their needs met.

Once this portion of the introductory meeting is complete, hand out information you've compiled about the networking group: a brochure if possible; if not, a typed up piece of paper outlining the networking group's goals, how often you will meet, and the location. You can also hand out Goal Sheets, which members will fill out and bring with them to the following meeting so everyone has a clear sense of each other's goals. Now is also the time to hand out the applications. The application gives the group a sense of formality and a sense of commitment. When people join and pay a membership fee, they are more prone to take it seriously. And you will need that because you want people to attend every single meeting. In fact, include a clause in the application stating your attendance policy. For example, if someone misses two meetings, membership can be revoked. Before the meeting is over, let everyone know the date and time of the first official meeting.

Here is a sample of a membership application and a goal sheet to my networking group, Women on the Fast Track:

Application For Membership

GROUP_____

Women
on the Fast Track

Date_____
Name_____
Company Name_____
Title_____
Address _____
Work Phone_____ Fax _____
Email_____ Website _____

The following will be used for distribution to members of Women on the Fast Track as well as posted on the WOTFT website.

Description of your business:

What are your objectives/goals of being a member of 'Women on the Fast Track'?

What other organizations do you belong to?

Return to: Women on the Fast Track
　　　　　2800 Utah NE
　　　　　Albuquerque, NM 87110

516.222.0236

Dues: $_____ per year. I understand that the number one "rule" or WOTFT is to show up. Two missed meetings in a row may result in your membership being revoked with no refund of dues.

Date joined _____
Check received _____

Defining your goals is a critical first step in reaching your goals. You should be as clear and specific as possible in describing your goals.

Before you can ask other people for help, you have to be clear in your own mind about what you need or want – just saying, "I want more business," is not enough to achieve your goals.

Please list your goals (desired outcome/action required).

1. _____
2. _____
3. _____
4. _____
5. _____

How will you measure your progress? (In other words, how will you know when you are on the right track to reaching your goals?)

1. _____
2. _____
3. _____
4. _____
5. _____

Who will be your accountability partners and when will you check in with them?

1. _____
2. _____
3. _____
4. _____
5. _____

Your First Official Meeting

The introductory meeting went well and you are now ready to proceed with your first real meeting of your new networking group. Congratulate yourself! You have accomplished something wonderful already and you are on the road to building a highly productive networking circle.

At this first official meeting, you will set the tone for all meetings to follow, so I can't stress enough the importance of having all your ducks in a row. Part of that is beginning the meeting at the designated time. It may be tempting to let people chat casually for a few minutes, but remember that you only have a certain amount of time to get through what you need to get through—and that's quite a lot, so stick to the schedule. As the founder of the networking group, it's up to you to welcome everyone in attendance. Then go around the room. Ask everyone to identify themselves, what they have to give, what they need. This part of the meeting should be interactive and energized. Encourage people to speak out and offer leads and other information to other members. But keep an eye on the clock—you don't want the meeting to go over your time limit. When it's time to wrap it up, thank everyone for attending. This may seem trite, but it's important to remember that showing appreciation goes a long way in networking.

Meeting Follow-Up

Within 24 hours, send a meeting re-cap e-mail to all of the members of your new networking group. It could be as informal or formal as you desire, but include as much detail as possible about what was discussed.

Sample e-mail:

From: You
To: My Network
Subject: Meeting Recap

What a fabulous meeting!

To re-cap our members needs for this month:

Barbara: Looking to connect with school superintendents within the Northern School District.

Sue: Seeking a printer to print her four color brochure

Tanya: Increasing her company's offerings to include financial planning for recently divorced men. Know any?

Beth: Developing a new clothing line to co-incide with her existing line. Looking for buyers in the upscale boutique market

Cynthia: Finished her television show pilot and would like everyones input on what could make it stronger.

Remember, stay in touch. Stay connected. See you next month. Same time. Same Place

---

Consecutive Meetings

The second meeting (which will resemble the third), should follow the structured format you set up in the first meeting. That means, the group leader (you) should welcome the group, then have everyone speak by going around the room. As each person has an opportunity to talk about any newsworthy events that happened since the last meeting, they should also be encouraged to ask for what they need, in terms of connections. But because networking is about giving and sharing, as each person is finished, open up the discussion so members can offer up their contacts. At this point, everyone should be taking notes. Let members know that this is important, because even if they don't have a contact to share at the moment, they might recall one back at the office. Or they might come across a piece of information that could be helpful to someone at the networking meeting, which they otherwise might not have even bothered to read (much less pass on).

At these initial meetings, you will likely begin to notice certain dynamics taking place. At first, the group will be in formation form, meaning, the group is just coming together, and people are getting to know each other, checking each other out. Then, don't be taken aback if there is some kind of disturbance among members—a confrontation or power play between two people who may want to emerge as leaders, for example. This disruption is normal and just part of the give and take that happens when a group of people get together. So don't worry, because once the group has taken on its own personality, you will notice the energy changing. Everyone will find "their space," and the group will become cohesive, working in unison and for one common goal.

The Path to Great Networking

Networking requires time and commitment, and while it may take a few meetings for everyone to warm up to each other, soon enough, members will be excited to see each other and will look forward to sharing news and contacts together. And ask for success stories to be shared at each meeting, so that everyone in the room benefits from hearing about connections that were made between group members. This will encourage everyone to persevere with their own networking goals, even if it takes a bit of time for their own needs to be met. And soon you will notice a sense of trust and goodwill developing right before your eyes. So before you know it, non-members will be contacting you about joining. I have found that it is best to allow an open meeting every six months for potential new members. But remember that you want to keep the group to a manageable number so that everyone gets to know each other's needs well.

As a Fast Track Networker, You Now Know:

- Starting your own networking group can seem like a daunting project, but by utilizing organizational skills and following a structure for the introductory meeting and follow-up meetings, you can do it. And you can do it in your very own, unique way.

- The first task is to come up with a dynamic name for the group. Next, find a great location and set up a convenient date and time for the introductory meeting. Determine who you will invite and set up a fee for membership. By setting a fee for membership, you also have to create a business structure for your new group, which means setting up some kind of formal corporation, opening up a business bank account, and maintaining accurate records for tax purposes. The good news is that you have complete control over how the money that comes in is used to build up this new venture.

- Create all of the materials you will need way ahead of time: press release, invitation, handouts, membership application, and so on.

- Encourage attendees to express their specific networking needs, rather than general goals. And set the tone via your leadership skills by keeping people on track if they swerve from specifics.

- During your follow-up meetings, make sure to check in on goals by asking how everyone is doing with theirs and seeing who might need support or assistance from the group. Promote dialogue by having everyone talk about their month. What happened? What was good? What successes did they have?

- Don't worry if a disturbance takes place among a few group members in the beginning stages, as this is normal when a group of people gets together. Everyone will soon find their place within the group and the magic will happen!

- Showing appreciation is imperative for continued sharing. So encourage attendees to offer a "Thank you" whenever possible at every meeting. The thanks will be appreciated and remembered by all.

I've often thought about starting my own group, and now I'm going to do it! I know it's going to be a lot of work, but the pay off will be enormous! I'm going to be the networking queen in my city.

—Amy Clithero, lecturer and senior program manager, Family & Community Medicine, UNM Albuquerque, New Mexico

FASTTRACKNETWORKINGFASTTRACKNE
KNETWORKINGFASTTRACKNETWORKIN
INGFASTRACKNETWORKINGFASTTRAC
ACKNETWORKINGFASTTRACKNETWOR
ORKINGFASTTRACKNETWORKINGFAST
STTRACKNETWORKINGFASTTRACKNETW
ETWORKINGFASTTRACKNETWORKINGF
GFASTTRACKNETWORKINGFASTTRACK
CKNETWORKINGFASTTRACKNETWORKI
RKINGFASTTRACKNETWORKINGFASTTR
TTRACKNETWORKINGFASTTRACKNETW
TWORKINGFASTTRACKNETWORKINGFA
GFASTTRACKNETWORKINGFASTTRACKN

Chapter Six

Network...Naturally

Let's take a moment now to pause and reflect on who you are when you are networking. Do you become a different sort of person when you are at a networking event or in business situations in general?

"Huh? I'm always me!" you say. However, if you really think about it, that may not always be the case. We wear all sorts of "masks" in business, whether it's to impress someone, to influence someone, perhaps because we are uncomfortable with our "real self," or maybe it's because we think we have to be someone other than who we are when we are out in the business world. But we don't. We need to be ourselves. And the reason why is that people connect with others on a level that isn't based on the mask we are wearing. We connect on a deeper level, an energetic level.

Have you ever met someone and within two minutes you know that you want to know them better? Have you met someone recently that you know, within an instant, would be a great person to network with? Have you ever met someone for the first time and known after the first conversation that you'd be friends? Chances are, most of us have, and these "gut reactions" aren't just formed because we think these new people can do something for us. The instant connection is formed because, most likely, they remind you of someone, of something, of a situation or an encounter that was good—and this person is bringing those feelings back to you! But if you are not being your genuine self, the real you isn't able to shine through. So how can you possibly make a meaningful connection with others if you're disconnected from the real *you*?

Being Yourself

To be a "natural networker" means that you come to every table, every room, every conversation, and every situation as yourself.

Easily said, but putting this into practice when walking into an event or meeting may take some time. And that's because networking events are, in fact, "artificial" environments. When you think about it, these are contrived scenarios in which a roomful of strangers are thrown together and expected to get to know one another. In complete contrast, a more organic situation might be bumping into someone at the supermarket, striking up a conversation and discovering that you have something of interest in common, and can even help each other. Now that's a genuine encounter, and who isn't completely themselves when shopping for groceries? At a formal networking function, you would probably act a little bit differently than at the supermarket. But with practice, you can be completely comfortable in your own skin, being exactly who you are, at all times, and wherever you are. A little self-talk and relaxation techniques can help.

Jennifer Urezzio, founder of the Intuitive Toolbox Program and founder of Know Soul's Language Program helps people understand their own innate insight and voice. And she offers a few practical tips that you can practice, so that your authentic self shines through whenever you are out in public.

Let's say you are getting ready to go into a networking function or event. Before you walk through the door, take a moment. You can do it in your car or at the entrance to the event—wherever you feel comfortable. Just shut your eyes for a moment and allow yourself to experience whatever you feel in your body: Do you feel tense? Then relax that spot in your body. Do you feel uncomfortable? Then try and understand where that's coming from. If it's coming from your unease about going into a room full of people you don't know, that's okay. Remember, they don't know each other, either. And they are all here for the same reason—to meet you! Does that still frighten you? It shouldn't if you consider who you are: a wonderful, interesting, intelligent person, a savvy business person, a parent, and a good friend to others.

So take a moment, and breathe deeply. Remind yourself of your strengths, successes, and accomplishments and that the people you are about to meet are excited to meet you and to get to know you.

Finally, take a moment to think about your real intentions for attending this event. Ask yourself who you are there to meet. Visualize people talking to you, exchanging information, and making plans to meet in a week or so. See yourself floating effortlessly from one conversation to another, smiling, and enjoying your time at the event.

By the way, these methods also work if you are going to a business meeting. Think about your intentions: Why do you need to meet these people? What do you have to give them? (And the answer is not the best rates on the copy machines you sell!) Who do you know that's going to make a difference in their business? Who can you refer them to?

When Shyness and Nerves Get in the Way of Authenticity

Sometimes people are not themselves at networking events because they are truly shy and nervous. I've had a lot of shy clients and shy business friends throughout the years who flat out said no way to networking. "I don't like networking, I don't feel comfortable in a room full of strangers," they've said. So I've brought them with me and introduced them to one or two people in the room and they've loved it. They just needed a little help, a friend, someone to break the ice for them. I know a brilliant young woman who works at a computer software company. She oversees hundreds of employees. She's responsible for much of the growth within the company, opening up different channels of sales, working with the sales directors to make presentations to prospective clients. In short, she is super talented at what she does. She had been to networking events in the past and told me how much she vehemently hated them. When I asked her why she felt that way, especially when there were so many industry functions that she could attend and contribute to, her answer was very simple: She didn't know what to say to the people she met without coming across like a salesperson. That was something we could work with, because at least she was aware of what made her feel uncomfortable. By working with her to help her realize that her attendance was a gift to the other attendees, and that she could help them with her knowledge and expertise, she was able to go to a big industry event with me where she met the chairperson of the event. She was then invited to sit on a steering committee for an association that was dedicated to furthering education within the tech industry. And once she approached networking as a way to give to the group, rather than a way to take, she felt released from her fears that she sounded too much like a salesperson.

Know this: You can be shy and still be great at networking. In fact, some of the shyest people I know are some of the best networkers as well, and that's because they don't want to take the limelight. They are quiet, but observant. They listen and that's a great skill. They are introverted and sometimes that makes for a very thoughtful person, one who builds relationships a little at a time. My point is, you can be shy and be genuine, and be a great networker all at once. Keep in mind that networking does not equate to being outgoing, gregarious, or the life of the party. It's more about being mindful, about thinking outside the box, about connecting. And this can occur whether you are outgoing or bashful.

I have a friend who is a forensic accountant. She is very quiet and humble. She is also very professional, and she rarely speaks, but she is extremely well-connected.

She knows all sorts of people and her clients respect her immensely. Believe it or not, she is in one of my networking groups. She shows up, she takes notes, and when she speaks, she is so quiet you have to almost strain to hear her. But when an organization I am involved in reached out to me and told me that they had an opening on their board for a treasurer, she is the first person I thought of. I introduced her to the president of the organization, they hit it off, and she accepted the board position. She is in her element. She now has the benefit of being connected to a great group, she has a leadership role on the board, and she is making all sorts of new business connections because she found a "fit" for herself and her personality!

Beware of Pretenders

Be aware of the types of networkers that you don't want to attract. You know you don't want needy people. Needy people in a networking relationship don't work. They suck the energy right out of you. Just as you don't want needy people in your personal life, you don't want them in your business life, either. You want to network with confident, assured people whose actions and words measure up and those who, like you, are truly themselves and comfortable with who they are, whether at the most casual social event or a high-visibility business function. And be aware of people who are not up front. These are not genuine people.

Suppose you are at an event. You own a business consulting company, you are very successful at what you do, and you have great clients. People know you, they respect you, they know your clients, and a lot of your clients are the best in their industry. You have the opportunity to introduce yourself and you do so, and afterward, during the mingling portion of the event, someone comes up to you and says he would like to get together with you to learn more about what you do. You take his card, you chat for another moment, and you agree to meet for coffee. As you are meeting for coffee a couple of days later, the conversation goes something like this:

Your New Contact: *Thanks for meeting with me. My company is a widget manufacturer that is the best widget manufacturer in the world, and I've been trying to get in to see Dave at TriTech (your client) for a really long time. Would you make the introduction?*

You are feeling a little upset, as this isn't why you thought you were having coffee today with this new contact. He said he wanted to learn more about what you do. What is this? You've been cornered by a pretender. So what do you say? This is a tough one. I've been there and it's not a nice feeling. I may have been inclined to make the introduction if my new contact had been upfront with me, but he was manipulative and not genuine in regard to how he got me to this meeting and cornered me. This is how you should address him:

You: *You know, New Contact, I would probably be willing to make the introduction to Dave at TriTech, but I need to know you a little better and I need to understand how you do business. Because when you asked me to meet, you said you wanted to know more about me and my business, which I believe you do, but the underlying reason you wanted to meet with me is to get an introduction to Dave, which I totally appreciate. But Dave won't appreciate it if I make an introduction to someone who isn't 100 percent up front with him. So* *tell me what you want to sell him and what you want to do with him and let's see if there's a fit.*

The reason I have no problem saying this to people who are not genuine is because I am highly protective of my contacts and clients. My reputation is at stake. And I am especially protective when a new contact comes at me sideways and isn't up front. That is not genuine.

You should try to avoid networking with people who aren't genuine if you can. People do business with people that they like, so why would you like someone who isn't genuine? I don't think that people are what they do, so when you can get people away from thinking that what they do is who they are, their genuine qualities do come out. Focus on the things that make these contacts human to you—are they married, do they have kids, where was their last vacation, what are their hobbies, what makes them tick? Now you are going to experience the real people...not their jobs. There is a woman who lives in the same city as I do. She is an older woman and is perceived as the "Mother of all things PR." She has been around a long time and knows virtually everyone in this city, in one way or another. Sound intimidating? Could be, but I took it as an opportunity to be in awe of her (and I am) and invited her out for coffee to get to know her beyond her reputation. She is fascinating. She isn't just a PR person; she is well traveled and well read. She has grandchildren that she adores. She misses her kids who live in another city. She is warm, genuine, and a really nice lady with a lot of interests. I've started to get to know the person behind the label of "Mother of all things PR" and I like her! Is she intimidating? Not in the least. She is a sage. She is delightful, and I don't think I would have known this had I just focused on what she does, rather than who she is.

I worked with a man for a while who ran the pharmacy relations department within a large pharmaceutical company. In his position, he had to appear very serious, strong, and capable, yet, underneath his serious job, he was really fun! He loved sailing. He was very active in his church. He coached his son's Little League and his passion was gardening. Once I got to know the genuine man, it was a lot easier to have a relationship with him and our business relationship not only grew stronger, but he started thinking about others within the pharmaceutical company that he could introduce me to, because he wanted to help me and help my business grow. We developed a strong connection, and we now enjoy both a personal and business relationship.

Attracting Genuine People

Like attracts like. Once you've made it a priority to be yourself and be genuine at networking events, think about the type of people you'd like to attract. Chances are, you're looking for the same type of up-front, honest, and down-to-earth networkers as you are. So be conscious when meeting someone for the first time. By being present and in the moment, you will then also be aware of how you feel when you are talking to a new person. Most of us are in "wait mode" until it's our turn to talk, but instead, be an active listener. Do you feel something as this new acquaintance is speaking to you? Is it positive or negative? Listen carefully. Does she spend all the time talking about herself and not asking you any questions? (Not asking questions is not a good sign.) In addition, note her body language. Is she looking you squarely in the eye as you chat, or is she scanning the room, ready to pounce on another person? Is she responding to what you say, or merely making superficial remarks? Does she seem as though she's ready to move on to someone else after just a few seconds of dialogue? Take note of all this —it requires effort but can ultimately save you time, grief, and misdirected energy.

Presenting Yourself

Although I always encourage people to be authentic at all times, including when they network, that doesn't mean be unprofessional. And being "natural" should *never* mean being inappropriate. We've all met the guy at the business meeting who speaks out of turn, who makes tasteless jokes just to contribute to the conversation and who in general, makes people feel uncomfortable. He's just being himself, you say. But there is a time and a place for everything. Here's an example.

I was recently a panelist at an event about networking with media. My panel included four distinguished professionals, all of them well-known and respected in media circles, and I admire them all. We all took turns answering questions from the audience, but while one of the panelists was responding, he used the "f" word. Needless to say, I am sure everyone was thrown for a loop. Granted, he was clearly passionate about the subject at hand, but in this kind of public forum, attended by professional industry people, his word choice was highly inappropriate. Was he being authentic? Totally. Did he make a poor impression on audience members? Absolutely. Is he someone you'd want to network with? Probably not. He may be well connected, but what if he uses offensive language when meeting some of your important contacts?

Here's another example of finding the right balance between authentic and professional: there's nothing I enjoy more than wearing comfortable clothing. Given the choice, I'd always opt for jeans and a sweater over a pair of tailored slacks and a jacket. And when I'm home, I feel my most authentic self dressed as such. But going to a business function requires wearing appropriate attire. I'm still my genuine self at these events and I'm confident that my approachable, friendly personality shines through, but at the same time, I always appear polished to the business world. So do be yourself when networking. Allow your persona to shine, but at the same time, adhere to the parameters that our business world sets forth.

As a Fast Track Network, You Now Know:

- By being your authentic self, people will want to connect with you on a meaningful level.
- When attending a networking event, in order to relax, remind yourself of who you really are and that the people at the event will like you, because you are a likeable, accomplished person. Also, if you feel tense, practice relaxation techniques such as deep breathing before entering.
- Beware of people who are not genuine. Look for warning signs: They cozy up to you. They call and say, "I would like to network with you, let's get together," and when you do, it's all about them and

how they want you to get them in somewhere, buy from them, do for them, and they don't offer anything of themselves.

- Sometimes it may not be obvious when a person you just met is not being genuine. But do try to be present and aware of how you feel when you are talking to someone new. Is this person someone you really want in your network? Is this someone who feels right to you? If your gut tells you this person doesn't seem authentic, her or she probably isn't!

- You can be a shy individual, or become nervous at events, and still be yourself and an excellent networker all at once. Don't attempt to cover up your natural shyness with non-stop chatter or nonsensical comments. People will read right through that. You won't be genuine. Instead, understand that it's perfectly fine to be quiet and introverted, but still be a giving person. Giving of yourself, your experience, your contacts, is what networking is all about. By being mindful of this at all times—rather than being mindful that you are uncomfortable in your own skin because you have to speak out at these events and meet people—your shyness will not be a hindrance. Allow yourself to listen attentively to others, but then reach out if you have a connection or information that they may find useful.

- You can be yourself without being inappropriate, so always follow social codes of behavior and conduct.

- We often judge books by their covers because the covers offer important information about the contents. So be authentic at all times, but also present yourself as a professional business person. If you don't appear polished, that is how you will be perceived, no matter how much you have to give the networking world.

- Above all, be yourself. Lose the fake "business mask" that you may be putting on, probably even without noticing it. You can usually spot someone who is "putting on airs" from a mile away. Other people notice, too, and will most likely be put off by the phoniness and seek out a more "natural networker" to talk to and do business with.

Through networking, I've met people who try too hard. They're overly friendly and overly pushy. I'm not comfortable networking with them because it's apparent to me they are not comfortable with themselves.
—Marcia Rosen, M.Rosen Consulting
Westhampton, New York

Chapter Seven

Hunters, Gatherers, Networkers

Talk to any businesswoman who has been networking for a period of time, and she'll reiterate my own observation: There are vast disparities between the sexes when it comes to networking, and you don't have to have a PhD in psychology to notice that men and women connect on different levels. In fact, there are differences between the way women network with men, in the way women network with other women, and in the way men network with other men.

Most women I've met are, for some reason, natural born networkers. My feeling is it's because networking is sharing and most of us have had it drilled into our heads from childhood that sharing is good; so we learned as kids to share our toys and things we had. This is good news, because as adults, sharing leads and sources becomes almost second-nature. An added component to that is that most women have a tendency to be givers—

we are very comfortable doing for others, giving to others, being available to others—which is a great trait to have. After all, giving is what networking is all about. As a result, women nurture our network. We become friends with the people we network with, because sharing is often an act that comes from the heart rather than from a bottom-line or deal-driven type of exchange.

What we aren't necessarily good at is receiving. We have a difficult time asking for help and receiving help, which is sometimes a hindrance to the networking process. As women, we also tend to downplay our abilities and we're not quite as comfortable as men in talking about our skills. We may be uneasy about highlighting our talents and when first starting the networking process, we may undermine what we have to give, thinking we aren't valuable enough, we don't know enough, and we just *aren't* enough. That's far from the truth, of course. But because women often operate on an emotional level, this is how we often feel about our capabilities and skills.

Men are, of course, operating on a different plane. As children, boys are typically more competitive than girls. Competitive means they want more; they want to be better; they want to win. So, from a young age, they have an "I deserve more, bigger, faster, better" mentality, which sets up an early, ingrained drive to win. Once they become men, they are task driven. They are bottom-line oriented, so they tend to want to make deals quicker and with less emotion than women.

Brad Stevenson, COO of Trans-World Dynamics who co-founded with Bob Sugar, LPC, CRET their "Power of Thanks" program, says that when men first walk into a room or a meeting, they spend the first several moments "posturing" for others. They stick out their chests, they spend time checking out the room, they zero in (like in the jungle) on their prey, and they stalk. In contrast, women walk into a room, and if they are confident in who they are, don't spend the time posturing, but do start looking for a place to belong. They spend their first few moments at the door looking to meet someone they resonate with. In other words, they don't treat a meeting or a networking event as a kill-zone or something that they are trying to conquer.

Networking Woman to Man

If you are a woman talking to a man at a networking event or starting a networking relationship with a man, you are going to approach it differently than if you are a woman meeting another woman. First, it's human nature to recognize that it's a person of the opposite sex. No doubt a sexual energy will be transmitted from both parties. In fact, I've seen professional women at the top of their game become giggly and girlish when faced with the prospect of developing a business networking relationship with a man. It's almost as though they are starting the "date me/choose me" type of dance. Their voices get higher, they stand closer to the man, and they may touch more. It's fascinating to observe because as their "dating approach" grows more noticeable with each subconscious gesture and subtle body language, their strength in business diminishes quite a bit.

Of course, this is not all women. I've also seen countless women successfully network without falling victim to the man/woman self-consciousness. However, I've witnessed enough networking encounters to have seen it time and time again, and it doesn't matter if the man is short, fat, balding, married, single, or drop-dead gorgeous. Some women act differently around men than they do around other women. And when women start their networking relationship this way, not only are they diminishing their worth, value, and strength, but they are also setting themselves up to be the lesser of the two in terms of business strength. They become the ones with less power and with less importance. The more they act as though they are in a dating game, the less seriously they will be taken, and the less likely that they'll get anything out of a networking event than possibly a few potential male admirers.

Hopefully, you are not one of those women; instead, you are savvy, smart, and have a solid back door strategy for networking with men. "Not always, but most often, men will launch into how terrific they are and that I cannot live without using their services," says author Elinor Stutz, CEO of Smooth Sale, a sales training company in California. "They give no thought to the fact that I am a sales trainer and may know some of the same information, at the very least. Ego gets in their way. When this occurs, I learned to walk up to the plate and hit a home run, so to speak. I acknowledge what was said, congratulate them on their success to feed their ego, and then blow them away with the fact that my published book sells worldwide. I don't stop there, but then tell them about all of my other endeavors."

This places Elinor on a level playing field. But what I often find works for me is to get the man to talk about himself. Yes, I'm stroking his ego, but by allowing him to "posture" right off the bat, we can then move ahead to what I really want to talk about—business and how I can help him connect to others in the room.

Now, according to Bob Sugar of the "Power of Thanks" program, men are predisposed to thinking about going into a conversation with a "what can I get" mentality. And when men find women to be assertive, confident, and eager, they begin formulating judgments about her. They may think for a woman, she's very pushy. Often, pushy translates to bitchy. Why does this happen? Sugar says that it's because in their collective unconsciousness, men feel they should at all times be in control and when they feel like they aren't in control, they feel threatened. So labeling a woman makes them feel better, and often even superior.

The truth is that, just like women, men are full of fear and insecurities. In fact, many men live with more fear than women can ever imagine. They may not admit it, but very often that is how they live on a day-to-day basis—with a deep fear of not looking good, not being able to take care of their family, not being good enough, not being able to live up to their fathers, and so on.

So when networking woman to man, remember that not only is the playing field equal, but you have more in common than you might think. Why is this important? "In networking, you must fully understand your audience in order to have any impact and a chance for doing business," Elinor Stutz adds.

Networking Woman to Woman

If you are a woman talking to or meeting another woman, most of the time the networking connection is going to begin with relationship building. Says Greater Milwaukee Area psychotherapist and owner of The Growth Coach, Gwen Nelson, "My sense is that... women focus their communication—even in a business networking environment—on personal information with the primary intention of building a relationship...We are hard-wired to do so. Men, on the other hand, may briefly engage a new networking contact in personal exchange, but typically quickly direct the conversation to business-related content. This fits much more naturally with the way men are hard-wired."

This is why at networking events, you will frequently come across women chatting about commonalities such as home, family, marital status, kids, clothes and, probably—even at the most high-level business function—hair. And by the way, there is absolutely nothing wrong with this approach, as long as building a relationship converts to building business at some point.

Man to Man

When a man meets a man for the first time at a networking function, the dynamics are poles apart. "The conversation is definitely different," says Vicki Donlan of Hingham, Massachusetts, a consultant, speaker and author of "Her Turn: Why It's time for Women to Lead America." In her experience, "Men are more likely to begin a conversation with a networking man with 'How about those Boston

Red Sox?' Men need only a one-liner to bond with other men they don't know. Men know that the other man is already a 'member of the club'—the old boys' club, and I don't mean that negatively. The boys' club is what gets men advancing up the corporate ladder and gets them the deal eventually." So men only need one opener and then they get right to the point of why they are there. They attend events with a distinct goal in mind. And adds Gwen Nelson, "They are not timid about communicating that part of the reason they are networking is to generate new business."

No Matter Your Gender... Authenticity Rules

Now that we are clear that there are differences in the way the genders network together, remember this: The best networking strategy for both men and women, no matter *who* you are networking with, is to be authentic. You can have a great product or service, but if you aren't you and people know that, chances are pretty good that they're not going to like you. And chances are even better that they're not going to want to do business with you.

When we come into a networking situation with our job as our identity, as opposed to letting our authentic personalities define our identity, it's more than a mistake. It's a door-closer. And although a large majority of both men and women in the business world may think that "what we do is who we are"—they are gravely mistaken and often miss the boat.

Whether men or women, the best networkers I know go into a networking situation and let their authentic personality shine through—leaving others with both a positive message, as well as a positive memory of them as the messenger. So leave the "dating hat," "competitive hat," and/or "inferiority hat" at home and chances are, you'll break down any gender barriers, letting in a barrage of new opportunities that you might not have otherwise explored.

As a Fast Track Networker, You Now Know:

- There's no question that men and women have different networking styles, and understanding these will help you connect to both genders.
- When women network with men, they should avoid behaving as if on a date, because this places women at a distinct disadvantage. Instead, relate to men on their terms by being friendly, but direct.
- When women network with women, they often need to build a relationship first. That's perfectly fine, as long as they remain aware that the goal is business related.
- When men network with men, generally, they just need an opening and then get right to the point. This serves them well, but they may want to alter that style when networking with women.
- Above all, regardless of your gender, be authentic— be yourself when networking and you will create successful connections, always.

*I get turned off when a man I am trying to network with
tries to flirt with me. It's demeaning, and steering him
towards the right track—that is, to business communications
exclusively—can take up valuable time that I don't
necessarily have to spare. However, it's a fact of life that in
order to be successful, men and women have to work together.*
—Lauren Frye, retail consultant
Palm Beach, Florida

Chapter Eight

Rein in Your "Deer in the Headlights" Approach

Once you have a good feel for networking and you've developed a solid flow of give and take with your contacts, you may ask yourself, "Now what?" Better yet, you *should* ask yourself, "Now what?" "What's next?" "What else can I do to continue networking effectively?" Networking is a prolonged, fluid process that should always be evolving.

Although one of the goals of networking is to become a more comfortable (and natural) networker, I always caution people about getting *too* comfortable when it comes to networking. So although you've probably made a number of valuable new contacts with your initial rounds of networking, the key is to continuously add new people to your network. You'll never be an ultimate networker—the go-to person who everyone wants to do business with and do business deals with—if you have the same people you keep referring over and over again. So continue to keep in touch with your contacts, continue referring business, but now it's time to expand your circle and add some more people to your network.

Inside Circle of 10

It all starts with what I like to call the "Circle of Influence" that you set up. For me, this is my inner circle of 10, my outside circle of 20. I like the number 10 and these are 10 business people that know my business as well as I do. They know it because they have made a point of learning exactly what I do (public relations and marketing) and how I do it. They value my work; they know what I want in a potential client. They "get me." More importantly, because they truly get what I do, they can perfectly capsulate my business and strengths when talking to potential new contacts for me. These are people that are my inner circle of 10. For me, 10 is about all I can handle because managing an effective network is work. It requires communication, care, and attention. It means taking an active role in helping the people in my inner circle with their needs, and we know this requires time and energy.

You may be wondering now how to select your inside circle of 10 people from everyone that you know. People that are in my inside circle of 10 are those that I naturally resonate with and who resonate with me. It's a natural synergy and a mutually beneficial working relationship. They are the people who I just click with in terms of networking and it's an easy relationship. Most of the time, I don't actually select them; instead, it happens organically. You meet someone, you get to know him or her, you start to refer business to him or her, he or she starts to refer business to you. You take your time in getting to know who his or her ideal client is, and he or she, yours. Those in this circle are never referred to as "I know someone who...." but rather with a glowing and assuring, "I have a very strong relationship with David, a printer who will take care of your printing needs in a timely fashion, will treat you fairly in terms of pricing, and I highly recommend him and his shop." You do more than refer them—it is almost as though you represent them as you represent yourself. That is how well you know their business. And that is how well they know your business. So without hesitation, you are working together to enhance each other's success.

Now, I don't think you need to necessarily tell someone that they are in your inner circle, but I do think they should know they are your: printer of choice, your marketing company of choice, your accountant, your restaurant, your hairdresser of choice. So that when David the printer gets a call from someone that I referred, and lands a huge account, my name will be top of mind—in his inner circle of 10—for a long time thereafter. And I can bet David will be calling me during that time to not only thank me, but to check in on my own business needs.

I talk to everyone in my inner circle of 10 at least once a week. I help them, and they help me. This sometimes goes on for a long time and as a natural, evolving process. It's not forced; they are there and they own my top of mind. And I can't tell you how many times a new lead or valuable new business contact has come from my own inner circle. Here's a great example:

Karen Dallago, owner of Dallago and Associates, a leading New York restaurant/hospitality design firm, called me after reading about my agency in a local magazine. She was interested in hiring a public relations agency. I met with her and her sister Sharon, who is her partner, and was immediately struck by not only how great their firm was, but how many amazing contacts they had. They knew everyone in the hospitality industry. They had a waiting list of clients who were willing to pay whatever it took to get Dallago and Associates to design their space. Now, I could have said, "Hey, you know so many people, how about opening some doors for us? We do hospitality PR." But that wasn't the way I was going to start a relationship with them. They ended up not hiring us, but they didn't hire anyone else, either. They just decided it wasn't the right time for them to work with a public relations firm. We kept in touch every once in a while. During this same period, I was writing a column called "Million Dollar Woman," for a local magazine. The column highlighted different women in the area who ran fabulous businesses. It was a column about what they did to succeed, what they did in the community, what their tricks of their trade were, and I decided to call Karen and Sharon and see if perhaps I could interview them for an upcoming column. This was my second meeting with them and they were very excited. When the article was published, needless to say, they were thrilled. It was a full-page piece with their photo and they loved it! We still weren't doing business together, but that was fine with me. I still believed there was opportunity here and I was also convinced that one day we would find a way to work together. Then about three months after the article ran, I got a call from one of our reporter friends saying that they were looking to profile a company that was "under the radar" yet still very successful—an up-and-coming business. I could have offered up one of our existing clients, as we had a lot of them that hadn't been profiled in this particular business paper. And being in PR and marketing, that would have been the logical thing to do—but I used this occasion to again go back to Karen and Sharon with this opportunity. You see, I was building a case as to why we were the best PR agency in the hospitality world and what better way to show them what we did, than to actually do it! So once again, they were profiled in this very visible business newspaper and once again they thanked me. Karen and I were also starting to become somewhat friendly outside of this business relationship and not too long afterward at a breakfast she said to me, "I've been waiting for the right time to do this, but I have a client whose name is John. He owns a food distribution company and he is a super guy. A super business person. Just an all round great man and I think the two of you would hit it off." She arranged for a meeting with me and Mr. John King, the "KING" of all things hospitality/food in New York. Karen was right—John was the key to all good business on Long Island. Not only did we did hit it off, but John hired us to do some work for his company. Then, he opened the flood gates to his customers by repeatedly stating to them, "I work with the best PR and marketing firm in the world." He tripled our business by spreading our name to his customers, as we had the opportunity to refer business to him. We still haven't done business directly with Dallago and Associates, but Karen was responsible for the networking connection of all connections and it was because in the beginning, I saw an opportunity to develop a relationship with her that yes, took time, yes, took effort, but no, I didn't know if it would ever pay off. But in the end, I had a very close friend and a fabulous networking referral source, who also now happens to be in my inner circle of 10.

Outside Circle of 20

Right outside my inner circle of 10 lays another key group for me, and that is my outside circle of 20. These are people that used to be in my inside circle of 10—remember networking is supposed to be fluid—and they are still valuable networking contacts and referral sources. I still do for them and they still do for me, but I don't talk to them weekly. They aren't people I'm developing relationships with; they are people I already *have* relationships with. They are set. It's all good. They are there and need care, like all relationships, but not as much as the circle of 10.

Circle of Influence

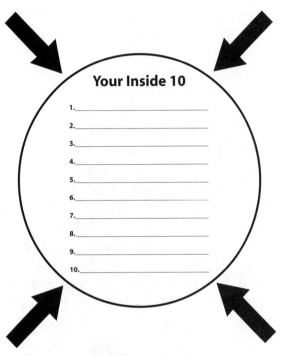

Your Inside 10

1._____
2._____
3._____
4._____
5._____
6._____
7._____
8._____
9._____
10._____

Your Outside 20

1._____	11._____
2._____	12._____
3._____	13._____
4._____	14._____
5._____	15._____
6._____	16._____
7._____	17._____
8._____	18._____
9._____	19._____
10._____	20._____

I'm sometimes asked if I keep an actual spreadsheet or file with my inner circle of 10 and outside circle of 20 people. I do not, because I have been networking for a long time, so keeping track comes naturally to me at this point. Certainly if it helps you, keep a chart of people who are currently "Top of Mind" in your own circles of 10 and 20. It can't hurt to have their names visible to you as you go about your own daily workload. But you have to remember that this is an evolving, flowing process. Your inside circle of 10 and outside circle of 20 is a natural movement. As you meet people and do business with them, you obviously can't have an ongoing relationship with all of them every day, every week. You may do a lot of networking with one person for a while and get to know them, like their work, and then meet someone else in the same field. Why start referring to this new person? Because this new person has contacts that they too can share with you, and that's how you expand and grow your circles.

Everyone Else

Outside of the circles of 30 or so are all the others. These are people who are absolutely, positively, part of my network, but as you can see, my network is constantly evolving and changing. I have contacts that I don't speak to for two years, but all of a sudden, I meet someone who needs what they do and I can refer them. Also, and this is important, often times there are overlaps in businesses. Who doesn't know a bunch of financial planners or business attorneys? We all know at least four or five. If you don't, you want to, because what if Susan is looking for a financial planner, but Susan is a bit difficult? You know she is difficult, you know she is demanding. You know it's going to take a special type of professional to work with her. So wouldn't it be nice to have a couple of different people to refer to her that you believe will be the best fit?

The Outsiders

Remember this: You can never know too many people. You can, however, know too many people who don't know how to network. "I won't introduce someone until they've proven to be quality," says Nick Pinkston, founder and CEO of CloudFab based in Pittsburgh, Pennsylvania. He clearly learned to filter for others from a past personal experience. "Someone introduced me to a bad contact once that wasted hours of my time on worthless products—thinking this person was a close friend of his. Later I was told that he barely knew him."

People who don't know how to network don't filter out poor connections. Instead, they'll refer you to just about anyone, and refer just about anyone to you. They don't take the time to really think through what makes a good connection—and they *never* ask you what you need. They take your contacts, they take your time, and they show up everywhere and rarely give. These are not people you want in your circles or anywhere near your network, for that matter. These are energy sucking people who only look out for themselves. These are the ones that have a pocket full of business cards and never ask for yours.

Take time out every once in a while to evaluate the people in your various circles, as well as the outsiders who may be ready to make their way inside. Also, make sure to regularly evaluate the networking groups and organizations you've joined, and see if they are in fact working for you. It's so easy to get caught up in just going to meetings, talking to people, and working your contacts, that sometimes we don't even realize if these experiences are helping anyone.

The Right Stuff

The only way to determine which networking groups are right for you is just like dating—you've got to try them on. You've got to attend as many networking functions as you can, as many groups, as many industry meetings as you can. And by attend, I don't mean just show up and observe. You have to go in ready to network. You must give freely. Otherwise, if you are holding back, it's impossible for you to figure out what works and what doesn't.

In my experience, it takes at least three months of a weekly networking meeting to see if there is a fit and/or if business is going to start coming your way. However, if you go into a networking meeting and everyone there is cold, not welcoming, and pretty much makes you feel unwanted, use your common sense: this is not a place for you!

"I research the group ahead of time to find out its makeup, who the power players are, what general theme or business segment dominates the group," says Michael Gall, president of The Gall Group in West Melbourne, Florida.

Researching groups is an excellent way to determine which ones to try out, but you really do have to go to all of them, and without expecting anything in return for a while. Remember, one of the keys to networking is to focus on giving, so you may not see direct results for some time. You have to go to the meetings, talk to the members, observe, and see how it feels to be there once you are there. You can call the organizer and ask if their group is made up of business owners, marketing executives, people looking for jobs, to change careers, salespeople, because there are all sorts of groups out there and they are all designed for a specific reason. I once read in the paper of a group that was called The Women's Entrepreneurial Network. Sounds great right? Sounds like a lot of women entrepreneurs; just up my alley and the perfect place to meet other women in business. They were having a lunch network meeting and instead of calling the organizer and asking what type of women in business attended, I just called and made my reservation and went. Then I found out that names can be deceiving because the entire membership was made up of women who were in business, but in the multi-level sales business, and that's who was in the room! Not my market. Not my clients' market. So it wasn't appropriate for me to be there at all. Did I meet nice women? Absolutely! Could I develop networking relationships with any of them? Doubtful, as most network marketers are trained to go after people to become part of their team or to buy from them. Every single woman in that room tried to push their cards on me and their sales literature. Very few asked what I did; they just wanted to know if I had heard of the company they represented. That's not networking.

Now for some, being in a room full of network marketers would be appropriate. But I should have done what Michael Gall does—had I researched the group ahead of time a little more thoroughly, I would have found out who was going to be there and I would have made an informed decision rather than just blindly attending because of what sounded like a good name for a network group.

In addition, if you join a group after it's already jelled and they are already in the networking groove, you are going to be the new kid. And just like when you went from grade school to middle school and you were the new kid, you've got to find where you fit in. Of course, in order to find out where you fit in, you have to dive in head-first and do your thing. Do not hold back! Give it your all. The worst that can happen is this: you go to a group for several months, give and give, but find out it's horrible, or the people you've been giving to are takers and don't know how to network properly. At that point, just stop going. Cut your losses and leave. You can't change people's mindsets most of the time, so if it's not going to work for you, if there isn't a click after a while between you and the group, why stay? There are plenty of other groups out there and you will find one that's right for you.

Finding Events

Pick up your daily newspaper and you're sure to see weekly—if not daily—listings of all sorts of networking events happening in and around your community. There are so many, in fact, that it may be difficult for you to choose among the many options out there. To narrow it down, ask some of your trusted business advisors (your accountant, attorney, financial advisor) which groups they attend. Ask other businesspeople you know. Post a query on Facebook and ask your friends and connections for their recommendations.

Formulate specific objectives for yourself before you attend even one meeting, so you are giving yourself a plan of action to follow. This works very well in narrowing down the options; after all, there are hundreds, maybe more, of networking groups in every town! Setting networking goals has helped, "me figure out what networking I should be doing, what industries I should be connecting with, as well as how to do targeted networking... spending time with the right type of network instead of just networking everywhere," says Taylor Ellwood, a business and social media coach in Oregon.

If that doesn't work, just pick one and go. I used to date a guy who had a favorite saying: "There is a seat for every a--." I think that applies to business networking. You are going to find your tribe. You are going to find a group that you resonate with.

Finally, keep an open mind when it comes to networking. You don't have to belong to formal networking groups only. In fact, charitable organizations, civic groups, Chambers of Commerce, church groups, sisterhoods, Civitans, Knights of Columbus, Lions Clubs, and other organizations throughout your community are also a fabulous way to meet others with a like mind. You are going to find people that share your sense of purpose in business. And when you do, it's not only a great feeling— it's magic.

As a Fast Track Networker, You Now Know:

- Networking is an ongoing, continuous process that should never come to a halt. If it does, people will not want to network with you any longer, as you will always be referring the same people over and over again. Just as every single business needs to grow by adding new customers or new clients to its roster, so does networking. To avoid stale referrals and connections, you should constantly ask yourself what else you can do to build up your network. And then reach out and take action.

- By creating your own "circles of influence," groups of 10 and 20 people who you are fluidly network-ing with, your connections will always be develop-ing, and your contacts will never dry up. Keep tabs on these important circles. Check in on the people within your various circles and as you meet new contacts, move them in and out of your circles of influence. Don't force this though—this is always best when it's a fluid and natural progression.

- Filter out takers; people who don't know how to network and who just want to use you for your connections without ever offering theirs. Remember; networking is a mutually beneficial working relationship.

- Take time out to take inventory of your contacts once in a while, so evaluate your connections as well as the networking groups you belong to. This is important, because it's easy to get caught up in groups without really taking note of their value. If they are not working for you, try something new. There are plenty of options out there.

- There is no getting around it; to find the networking groups that are right for you, you can research them ahead of time, but you must go to the meetings. And you can't just be present; you must be active. There is no other way to determine if you and the group mesh. You can't possibly know if a new contact is a true networker (a giver) unless you network with him. If it doesn't work out, move on. There are plenty of great networkers out there just looking to meet someone like you.

- If you can't find a group that works for you, think outside the traditional networking box. There are non-profit organizations, charitable organizations, civic groups, and other places for you to look into. Check them out and you may be surprised to find that these are a better match for your specific needs or personality.

One of the things I've learned about referring people over the years is to be generous, yet cautious. In other words, I won't refer someone I just met two seconds ago to someone that I've been networking with for years. You need to know who all the players are—otherwise, your reputation can easily be put to the test!
—Christina Eyuboglu, president, Leverage
Communications
Wilmington, North Carolina

FASTTRACKNETWORKINGFASTTRACKNE
KNETWORKINGFASTTRACKNETWORKING
KINGFASTRACKNETWORKINGFASTTRAC
ACKNETWORKINGFASTTRACKNETWOR
ORKINGFASTTRACKNETWORKINGFASTT
STTRACKNETWORKINGFASTTRACKNETW
ETWORKINGFASTTRACKNETWORKINGFA

Chapter Nine

Not Working? Try Networking

One of the most awkward situations for a person to be in is to be unemployed…and networking. Yes, if you are seeking a new position, you still need to be networking. In fact, there is no better time! You may feel as though you have nothing to give, therefore, why should you be networking? Not true, and definitely not the right mindset (and certainly not the positive attitude you should be having during a job search). In fact, some of my best networking success stories have come from helping some of my unemployed networking contacts find new jobs. These are people who have consistently gone on to either refer me to *their* new company for business, or to put me in touch with others they know (and will continue to meet). People never forget a favor and they never forget a person who goes out of his or her way to help them with no strings attached.

Seeking New Employment

Just because you don't have employment now, doesn't mean that all the people you've "collected" through the years suddenly vanish. You will get a job, you won't be out of work forever, so think about connecting with people from other places where you've worked, people whom you've worked with, your church/synagogue, your children's contacts, your spouse's contacts. Just because you are out of work doesn't mean you have to be out of the loop and out of touch with others. In fact, so often people who are out of work tend to focus on their need to get a job, that they can't seem to see beyond that and miss out on some great opportunities to make some new connections that can help them in the future. Remember, networking isn't about what you need, it's about give and take, so be sure to still be giving. You can do this as you are going on interviews and applying for jobs. You may hear of an opportunity that you don't qualify for, but that you can share with someone else. Sharing what you are discovering out there keeps you connected. And being connected still remains one of the top ways to get a new job and make some new contacts (and friends) in the process.

Out-of-the-Box Networking

You know that a new job won't come knocking on your door, so in addition to the standard job-seeking resources out there (classified ads, employment agencies, etc.) and networking with people you know, try to think out of the box. That's just what Jack Goldenberg of northern New Jersey did.

"Even though I played a strategic role in marketing four billion dollar products (McDonald's Happy Meal, Cabbage Patch Kids dolls, Pop Rocks candy, and instant scratch-off state lottery tickets), I was out of work for almost a year in 2008 after Bristol-Myers Squibb let go of about 10,000 freelancers and full-time employees," he recalls. But after about eight months of being unemployed, he says he figured out a great way to network himself into a new job. "I spearheaded my Phi Epsilon Pi (American University) fraternity reunion. What better way to contact over 100 men who felt an affinity toward me because we were in the same college fraternity?"

Goldenberg took charge of the organizing and along with three fellow frat brothers, they contacted 182 men, 80 of whom ended up attending the three-day reunion in Washington D.C. "One of them hired me, which eventually led to my current job as Director of Social Media Marketing for Zytrel XP; the world's first extended protection hand sanitizer."

Connecting with people from the past worked wonders for this savvy networker and today, it's easier than you think to get back in touch with people from your past who just may be able to shape your future. Thanks to social media sites such as Facebook and LinkedIn, you can look up former colleagues by name or business and reintroduce yourself to them. I know someone who was recently laid off from her job in finance. She had no hesitation about posting a comment on her Facebook page, to let all of her friends know that she is out of work and to please keep their eyes open for someone with her qualifications. I have no doubt that in no time, she will have a new position, because who better to recommend her than the people who know her best?

In addition, read your alumni publications closely and take note of former classmates and friends you've lost touch with who may be in your field (or who may be good overall contacts). Don't be shy about letting them know you are out of work, because chances are, if they can't help you directly, they know someone in their business circle who can.

Let the World Know

There's no stigma to being unemployed—everyone knows someone who has been laid off, whose company has shut down or severely downsized. So there should be no shame in letting *everyone* you know that you are seeking a job—from fellow parents on the PTA to the barista at your local coffee shop (you just never know who knows someone…) and when spreading the word, being very specific about what you are looking for will help you land a new job. So instead of saying "I'm looking for a job in sales," say, "I am looking for a job in Internet advertising sales. Do you know anyone that is in charge of online advertising at so and so Websites?"

Use Free Time Wisely

It's worth stating here that another great place to let people know that you are seeking employment is at your networking meetings. You may not feel like attending any networking meetings if you are out of work, and that's somewhat understandable. But it's a proven fact that the best jobs are ones that come from insider knowledge and direct referrals, not from newspaper classified ads. I'm not discounting career search firms, and such, but it's a lot easier and a lot more effective if you are referred to a specific company for a job opening or if one of your networking contacts makes a call to the HR person or hiring manager for you. If you can approach looking for a job as you would any other networking situation, you'll be ahead of the game. So motivate yourself to go to events, outings, and meetings by realizing that you don't want to be "out of the loop" in terms of connections and contacts, because once you do land a position, you don't want to have to explain to your groups where you have been for the last few months. If possible, landing a new job should be a seamless transition.

While you are at your networking meetings, you may not get a chance to tell every single member of your group individually that you are seeking new employment, so ask the group leader if you can make a quick announcement either at the beginning or the end of the meetings. When doing so, use your elevator pitch to remind members what you do. In addition, tell them how long you have been in your particular field, and even offer up a few brief success stories. Hand out your cheat sheet so people can take it back with them. And ask the group leader if they can add a quick reminder in the follow-up newsletter or other materials. The bottom line is if there is one occasion in which it's perfectly appropriate to sell yourself in a networking situation, this is it.

In addition, utilize your free time to identify people within the industry you want to work in, people that are at the top of their game, and request a 20-minute meeting with them. You'll be surprised at the positive responses and I'll tell you why you will very likely be welcome for these brief meetings: because smart businesspeople are always networking, whether at an event, or at their own office. They know that frequently meeting new people is the key to success, and sparing a few minutes in the middle of their workday is an effortless way to do so!

The meeting should not be utilized to sell yourself and to land a job. Instead, the meeting should focus on the industry you are interested in. So be honest when you set up the appointment—state that you are job hunting within their industry and although they may not have a position available for you, you are seeking their counsel about the industry, your skills, and your qualifications. Ask if they would theoretically hire you. Show your resume and ask for them to critique it. Then take their input to heart. If they tell you that you don't have the necessary skills to do the job you are applying for within their industry, use this time productively to go and learn the skills. And remember this: Once you get an appointment with someone within the industry you want to work in, you've made an important networking contact. Treat it as such by sending a thank-you note after the meeting. Most importantly, you should stay in touch with this contact on a somewhat regular basis. Let them know what you are doing, let them know if you found a job, if you hear about something within the industry that may be of importance to them.

Finally, while you are unemployed, it's always a good idea to sign up for volunteer work—all of your free time should not be devoted to your job hunt. You never know, by reaching out to help others, you may just connect with someone who can help you find a new job.

Helping the Jobless

Chances are, you've been (or will be) on the receiving end of someone out of work who wants to network with you. Help them (and I can't stress that enough). This isn't the time for you to shut the door on them because they can't help you. Being out of work is terrifying, and if there was ever a time that this person needed networking support, now would be it. And I promise, not only will your good deeds and good contacts help someone else, but they'll come back to help *you* ten-fold.

"I make it a point to help people out," says Jennifer Dunphy Rzasa, VP of Sales and Marketing at Vayu Media in Atlanta, Georgia. "About nine months ago, I made a connection with a woman that I met that was looking for a job. After a few interviews, she was offered the position. Being grateful, she ended up calling me a few months later with an account that she pretty much sold for me and it was a sizable account. All I had to do was go in and run through the proposal and get the agreement signed!"

Here's another example of networking—or "pay it forward" networking at its best. We had a client that was a huge manufacturing company and the director of marketing (our point of contact) was fired. I had a feeling that he was going to have a rough time finding another position that paid well in his field, because director of marketing jobs are somewhat coveted positions. I helped him find someone to re-write his resume, I invited him to networking events with me, I spoke to him on the phone every month or so, and I sent him encouraging e-mails. I also introduced him to several business owners—none of them were necessarily looking to hire a marketing professional, but

I made the introductions in case they knew other companies that were. His job search took over a year, but he kept on persevering and we kept communicating. I always took his phone calls, and even though I wasn't responsible for finding him his next position, he remembered that I cared. So when he finally landed a position as a marketing director, he brought us in to pitch his new company. And since he was in charge of marketing, he had the ultimate say in who got the account. Needless to say, we did.

Of course, this shouldn't be the reason you help out someone who is unemployed. But do keep in mind that this is really a small world. You never know if the unemployed account executive you snub today will be tomorrow's head of operations within a company you have been trying to sell to for years.

Changing Careers/Paths

At some point, you may decide to change career paths: You don't want to be in banking anymore; you don't want to be a mortgage officer anymore. You can't stand the thought of doing what you've been doing day after day for one more day. Still, you feel glued to your chosen career and have no idea how to detach and move into an entirely new direction. How do you go about being a river raft guide or a portrait photographer? How do you go about breaking into an industry in which you neither have experience or contacts?

It's not easy...but it certainly isn't impossible. First, write out an action plan to outline what you need to do in order to get into the industry you want to work in.

Next, start doing your research. There are industry associations for just about every trade under the sun; all you have to do is be clever in finding them. The Internet (obviously) is the place to start. Search every keyword you can think of that has to do with the industry you want to be in and get the information from the organizations/associations that pop up. Subscribe to their online newsletters. If there is a local chapter, think about attending one of their meetings. Start reading everything you can about the industry you want to go into and start talking about what you want to do with the people you know. Be assertive in your search, ask questions, and dig deeper. If there is something you need to learn to be in this new field, go take a class...but by all means, start talking to others about what it is that you want to do so they can start helping you by opening doors for you. So make a list of who you know that is either in this industry or connected to this industry. Would they be willing to meet with you for a cup of coffee? Be honest with them in what you are looking for, be focused when you meet with them, be clear about what you want, but don't take up tons of their time. And of course, thank them time and time again.

Networking Action Steps For a Career Change

Subscribe to free e-mail newsletters, rss feeds and blogs in your field of interest	Work part-time in a field that interests you
Send interesting articles to those in your network	Talk to professors at your college/university
Join an Association in your field of interest	Go to school and set up an internship or practicum
Talk to the head of an association in your field to gain insight and "get current" on the industry	Work in a related area where you can learn and explore skills and broaden your network
Ask family and friends for contacts to informational interviews	Shadow someone doing the job you're interested in
Volunteer	Read the newspaper and industry blogs everyday to stay current
Get and distribute business cards	Keep your resume up-to-date and focused
Set up a professional email name	Find a Mentor in your industry
Set up a professional voicemail message	Interview people in the job you want
Follow and interact with industry leaders on social media platforms	Subscribe to and read company white papers that interest you

There was a young woman who worked for us a few years ago. She was bright, articulate, and very nice. She did her job well at the agency, but she really wanted to be a news reporter. She was a brilliant writer and although I loved having her write our clients' material, I also knew she wasn't fulfilled. So we talked and decided she was in almost the right field, but not quite—her heart was really in reporting. So I made some calls for her and got her a position as a reporter at a local paper. I don't need to tell you how great it is for a public relations agency to have a friend at a local paper. Later she was promoted to editor at that paper and soon after landed a new position as a reporter at a national publication. Have we kept in touch? Absolutely. Does she take my calls? Always. Did it take a lot of effort on my part? Not really. Yes, it took some thought and perhaps it took some time...but was the effort worth it? Without a doubt. And I'd do it again in a heartbeat.

A man that I know was a post office employee for more than 20 years. He recently retired, but he now wants to work in a pharmacy. He would love to go back to school (at age 55) and get his pharmaceutical degree, but for now, he needs a break into the pharmacy world. I know pharmacists, but that may not be the ticket to get him in. I thought about this man for a couple of days; really thought about him, and then I realized that I know a couple of pharmaceutical reps, people that have direct contact with pharmacists and pharmaceutical companies. I am working on putting him in touch with them, hoping that something happens for him. Why? Because it's the right thing to do. And because I truly believe in the power, and promise, of networking.

Make Time for Others, Always

Always make time for people.... Always. Always. Always. That is what networking is about and also because you just never know where they are going to end up, job-wise. Another young man who worked with us was a very clever public relations person, very full of energy, and overall a great guy. But he was an entrepreneur at heart. He was a young man who needed to be working with entertainers and performers, none of whom my company represented. I helped him make a plan for a new business, pushed him out the door, and told him to fly. At the same time, I gave him all sorts of media contacts, and yes, kept in touch. During the first year that he was on his own, he would periodically e-mail me with questions about various issues he came across: what I thought, if he should/shouldn't, etc. and I always answered. This young man now represents some of the biggest rising stars in the entertainment industry. He now sends *me* contacts, and e-mails saying, "If I can help you, let me know." And I do! A lot!

By making time for someone, there is a good chance that they will, in turn, make time for others. Maybe it will be you, maybe it will be someone else, but that really doesn't matter, because it's a positive, pay-it-forward kind of energy. Once someone experiences you giving to them unconditionally, chances are they are going to want to do the same for someone else.

As a Fast Track Networker, You Now Know:

- Don't stop networking if you are out of work. You still have your history, which means you still have connections to offer others. In fact, this is where networking is a necessity. So even if you feel down about being unemployed, make every effort to attend as many events and groups as you can. This will make you feel good, because you will be helping others and you will be utilizing your free time in a very productive way.

- Creativity can help you land a dream job. So do think outside the box when job hunting. That means contacting people you grew up with, old colleagues from previous positions, college friends, members of your PTA...the list is endless.

- Use social networking groups to make connections with new people and to let people you know that you are seeking a new position.

- You have time to set up 20-minute meetings with key people in your desired industry, so call them. Be honest about why you want to meet, and stress that you are not looking to get hired at their company, but rather to talk about the industry in general and about your skills in particular. Once you do this, you will have made valuable new networking connections that you can contact periodically, and in the future, when you have employment once again.

- Always make time to help others who are unemployed. It's just the right thing to do—and you never know how that person may pay it forward by helping you out one day. So accept calls from people who don't have jobs; take time to have a cup of coffee with them; take a few minutes out of your day to call a connection in your circle of influence about any openings for your unemployed contact. Even if you don't directly help him find a new position, you will feel good about lending a hand and showing your support. More importantly, you will make the person feel worth your time—even if he or she doesn't hold a job at that moment.

- There is no shame in being unemployed. So inform everyone you come into contact with that you are seeking a job, and be very clear and specific about what you are looking for. And remember to announce it to every networking group you belong to, reminding members what you do.

- Doing good for others simply feels good, so seek out volunteer opportunities while you are searching for work. You might even offer your valuable skills to non-profit groups or organizations. Are you an accountant? Ask if they need help during tax season. Do you have an ability to write press releases? Can you give a few hours to a reading program for youngsters? How about visiting an elderly person in a nursing home? What about offering your services for free to a food pantry seeking donations? The possibilities are endless.

*Before I really understood the value of networking, I avoided
jobless acquaintances like the plague. I guess I didn't see
the point. But these days, there is no such thing as job
security. That's why now I try to help in any way that I can.
Everyone might lose a job, and everyone needs a helping
hand to find one under pressing economic circumstances.*
—Philitha Stemplys, owner, Ona Lucia Photography
Granby, Connecticut

Chapter Ten

Facebook...and LinkedIn... and Twitter. Oh My!

In a world that is moving at the speed of light, it's difficult to know when it's time to hop onto the newest technology train, or when to just wait for the next one to come along. In the case of social media (Facebook, Twitter, LinkedIn), the decision to jump on the latest trend is even more difficult. Unlike a Website or online advertising, the time and education needed to commit and stay engaged in the social media world can be slightly overwhelming. But the alternative—choosing *not* to climb aboard the social media bandwagon—can not only result in you seeming a little outdated in terms of your peers, colleagues, and potential new contacts, but can prove to significantly limit your networking success, as well.

More Than Your Friends.
It's Your Brand.

It's true that past generations of business professionals were quite successful without ever being concerned about how many "friends" they connected with on their online business profile, or what their next "tweet" should say about an upcoming business event. That's simply because social networking didn't exist. But in today's world, everything has changed. As some of the most successful marketers can tell you, if you use the platform of social media and social networking strategically, you can build an online presence that will not only enhance your other marketing strategies, but will possibly replace them. In addition, social networking can help you monitor, build, and protect your brand, and/or the reputation of your business, as you grow and build your influence and share your expertise in today's marketplace.

According to Florida's Alison Berke Morano, a social media expert and president of Bworks.com, building an online network of customers, clients, and business associates should be as valuable a resource as your day-to-day networking in person, or on the phone. Although it may seem, on the surface, to be a passing fad, she stipulates that the value of social networking can be exponentially significant to your outreach into your own community, and have a global effect as well.

Consider the true core of networking. True networking is not just a face-to-face meeting with a new contact, who may or may not be a future client, lunch date, or even mentor. The number one objective to making a new contact is to ultimately become a part of their network. In other words, the goal is to not only meet one individual person, but to hopefully gain access to the full network of their contacts.

The same holds true for social networking. Through the power of the Internet, you are able to make one connection that not only gives you access to that person's network of friends, but that then can also allow you to touch an even larger network of friends-of-friends. And it enables you to "meet" people right from your desk. This has worked well for Pinny Cohen; managing director of New Jersey-based Pin Media. She says she's used social media to find people in her industry, marketing, and business consulting. Once they are identified, she follows their posts in order to learn about them, and when possible, offers helpful responses to their posts, which leads to friendly conversation. "Meeting people online and transferring it into an in-person meeting later will raise the odds of you sticking in the person's mind, and you should seek it out as much as possible," she advises.

With Twitter, you can reach and follow some of the most high-profile business leaders in the country, opening up some huge potential doors right from your PC or cell phone.

In today's fast-moving world, the value of social networking is in dispensing a great piece of information to a lot of people. Whether you are posting a status update in the limited amount of characters that Twitter allows (140 total), or a longer post using Facebook, LinkedIn, or your personal/corporate blog, today's Internet users are looking for information, news, tips, and updates. And, if you are sharing useful info, they will pass it along to others, giving you credit for the original idea or inspiration.

This, in turn, will likely prompt *their* circle of connections to seek you out so that they can receive your updates directly...and your social media circle (and amazing new contacts) will continue to grow by leaps and bounds.

Although the reports of business success using social media are just starting to be analyzed, there are already some great examples of how businesses and individuals are using social media to expand their customer outreach and business network. For example, says Alison Berke Morano, a business as large as a bank is just exploring the ways they can keep their followers updated on daily interest rates, or special programs they may be developing. And a business as small as a street vendor can develop a following by posting where they will be serving lunch that day. Individuals specializing in a specific industry can develop a very large following by posting tips on a daily basis.

All of these posting techniques operate on the same principal as keeping a Website updated, publishing a newsletter, or even giving a lecture at a local venue. All of these options are a great way to distribute information, and incorporating a social media strategy is the next step in getting the word out. So here are tips from my own social media guru, Alison Berke Morano, on how to make the most out of your social network.

Grab Your Name— Protect Your Brand

One of the first steps you should take in building your social media presence is to secure or register your company name or personal brand. Most social networking sites, like Twitter (*www.twitter.com*), Facebook (*www.facebook. com*), or Ning (*www.ning.com*) allow you to register or personalize your account with your own name when you create a page in their networks. Some websites have different requirements for gaining a personal or vanity URL (for example, Facebook pages require that you gain at least 40 friends before you can choose a personal URL), but most allow you to choose a user name that reflects your business when you register with them. You should also create accounts at some of the larger Websites, even if you won't be utilizing them right away.

Define Your Social Media Strategy

One of the most useful aspects of the Internet is that it allows you to do a great deal of research in a short period of time. So before you jump into a social media posting blitz, check out the competition. How are they using social networking Websites for their business? How many fans, friends, or followers do they have? What are they posting about? How often are they posting? And, if you do not see your competition in the social world, don't let that stop you. In fact, it should encourage you, as you will be a pioneer in your industry.

Once you have evaluated the competition, create a strategy for your business or brand. What is your objective? Is it to cultivate new business? Give advice to current customers?

Balance your postings with interesting information about your products and services. Offer advice and incentives to your followers (your network community). One thing you will learn early on, especially from reading posts from others, is to make sure your information is useful and interesting to your followers. It's astonishing how many people post mundane daily activities online. But for business, no one wants to know what you had for breakfast that morning. They do want to know the latest news and updates from your business or industry. They are also looking to learn from your years of experience and expertise in your field.

Also, make sure that in your social networking, just like in traditional networking, you leave out the sales pitch! Try to stay away from direct advertising, and make sure you offer advice in a useful, productive manner, rather than simply putting up an ad for your business. This will not only cost you your audience, but you may be removed from the service altogether since most social media sites sell direct advertising as a way to create revenue.

Remember That the Internet Archives EVERYTHING

Although you should not hesitate to jump into the world of social networking with both feet, be mindful of your online reputation. If you are going to have a social media editor or strategist update your online status, make sure he or she understands that he or she is overseeing your business, and responsible for your corporate (and personal) presentation to the online community. Create a good social media policy for your business, or to even follow yourself (there are several examples on the web already). Do not use profanity, personal attacks, or offhanded remarks, as these can be picked up by a myriad of people and search engines at any time. Remember that as fast as you can grow your brand online, it can also be hurt just as quickly.

Incorporate Links to Expanded Information in Your Status Updates

As with most headline news (status updates), followers always want more information on the topic you are introducing or discussing. Try to incorporate a link to the topic in your posting. Whether it's a link to the news article you are referencing, or a written post on your own blog, your followers will appreciate a way to get more information from you. In addition, you will find that status postings that include links and references are more likely to be reposted by followers, with your name in the reposting for credit. This then introduces you to the networks of your followers, friends, and fans.

Join the Conversation

A social network is not a one-way street. Rather than thinking of your social presence as an announcement-only-based system, do what the strategy implies: be sociable. Platforms like Twitter allow you to literally join in ongoing conversations by adding a keyword to your posting, preceded by the hash tag (#socialmedia). A list of ongoing conversations can be found on the Twitter Website. For Facebook, every posting allows for comments from that user's network. If any of your friends or fans posts a question or topic that you are knowledgeable in, add your comments to their posting. Search for blogs in your industry, or blogs that might be of interest to your potential contacts and customers. Participate in the conversations on those Websites. Your expertise will be welcomed by both the readers and the authors, as they usually welcome outside input and advice. Again—remember to follow proper netiquette guidelines—you do not want to alienate anyone that might be a current or potential contact!

LinkedIn

Although Twitter, Facebook, and other social media sites can boost your business, do not neglect LinkedIn for a professional presence. In the social media world, LinkedIn is where the professionals specifically congregate and "follow" their corporate contacts. While primarily an individual profile system (meaning you will be setting up a presence for yourself individually, rather than your company), LinkedIn allows you to describe your company and link your employees and contacts to your personal profile. From a corporate standpoint, other professionals use LinkedIn to find industry experts and business leaders. From a personal standpoint, LinkedIn provides individual leads and information in the business world.

Actively Market Your Social Media Presence

Much like the traditional marketing strategies you've employed for your business location, phone number, e-mail, and Websites, advertise your social media sites and URLs. Add your Facebook user name, and Twitter and LinkedIn profile pages to your Website pages, blog postings, and e-mail signature. Most social networking sites allow you to add coding to your Websites that will automatically integrate and embed these applications directly into your social media Web pages.

When You Post, Cue Up Your Keywords

If you do a search today on a Website like Google, Bing, or Yahoo!, you will begin to notice that the sites at the top of the results (following the sponsored ads), are coming from social networking Websites like Facebook and LinkedIn. In addition, the trend of these search engines is that they will be offering more and more search content directly from social media Website postings and status updates. Knowing this, it's important to utilize this technology and incorporate keyword, or "buzz" words into your postings. This will allow your postings to rise to the top of the general search engines when someone is searching for information in your field or specialty. Again — do not advertise. Provide information, but save the pitch for the right time/place.

Allow Your Followers to Participate

The same rules you are encouraged to follow when participating in other social media universe discussions, should apply to the conversations that arise from your own postings and status updates. Once in a while, you may have a negative posting or a complaint from a customer or even a competitor (possibly under a third-party poster). It is important that you do not panic if or when this occurs. If the complaint or comment is legitimate, use this as an opportunity to help solve the issue, or to open a dialogue that will help you create a better communication between you and your followers. If it does turn out that you cannot solve the problem, or that the person with the issue cannot be mollified, just move on. In some cases, you may even find that another follower will come to your rescue!

It Doesn't Happen Overnight—Give It Time

Although it's not a very good idea to start a blog or a running commentary on Facebook and then let it drop for weeks on end, remember that there are only a few cases where an individual or company has caught fire overnight, collected thousands of followers, and became the star of the social media scene. Just as in traditional networking, developing an online network of followers and creating an interest in your brand takes time. But it shouldn't take up all of your time. Some sites do require that you reach a specific number of followers before they will give you a personal URL, or vanity name, but for the most part, you can build a social network following by providing trustworthy information, good tips, and strategy, and by participating in the social dialogue. If you can only post semi-regularly, try to use the networks that do not require a time-consuming process in order to stay engaged. For example, a post on Twitter or Facebook is certainly easier and quicker than the upkeep of an in-depth blog. Take on what you can reasonably handle, and let it grow from there. You may be surprised to find that the other activities that take up your marketing time will be replaced by the value of keeping in touch with your social media network.

As a Fast Track Networker, You Now Know:

- Whether you like it or not, social networking is the way people are conducting business these days, so learn as much as you can and get into the game. Think of it as just a new and exciting way to add to your networking possibilities.

- By using social media and social networking strategically, you can build an online presence that will create a strong brand name for yourself and/or your business.

- Use social media such as Facebook to post interesting things about your business, and to connect with potential networking contacts. Follow various people's posts and don't hesitate to comment. But then do try to connect in person to build on that.

- Just as with traditional person-to-person networking, social networking requires a time commitment. Be patient, build your strategy, stick with it, and in no time you will have expanded your networking connections in directions you'd never even dreamed possible.

Facebook and Twitter have become a great networking tool for me and my business contacts. What I really love about it is that it's immediate—you send someone a private message, and you get a quick response. You post a question or a business need, and someone is bound to answer right away. It's amazing.

—Susie Shina, CEO, Gettin The Good Stuff
Atlanta, Georgia

Chapter Eleven

From Filofax to Your Digital Filing Cabinet

Consider this: How often have you attended a large networking event, collected dozens of business cards, and flung them into your desk drawer for future use? Or you placed an assortment of cards into your briefcase right after the event, only to find them months later along with receipts and old gum wrappers. Then, when you suddenly recall that you once met a small business accountant that would be a perfect fit with a new networking connection, you have no idea what the accountant's name is and can't find his business card.

One of the most common questions people ask me about networking pertains to organizing all of the great contacts they're making. This is an important subject, because knowing how to maintain contact information in a logical, functioning, and methodical fashion can make or break your networking experience. But first, answer this—do you still have a Rolodex sitting on your desk? I know plenty of smart businesspeople who still use this relic from the past. They attach their collection of business cards to individual Rolodex cards, and then keep them filed in alphabetical order—right next to their iPhones or Blackberries! To those of you who are guilty of this, it's time to kiss your Rolodex goodbye! One of the wonderful, amazing things about the computer age is that there is an application for just about every need, not the least of which is business contact maintenance. So in this chapter, we'll cover the basics to give you a clear idea of what you can do and what's possible when it comes to fool-proof ways to easily manage, and access, your growing list of contacts.

And while I hope that this information proves useful (and is certainly great, especially for those of you still in the Rolodex age), I highly encourage you to explore this subject even further to learn as much as you can about today's new data management technology. Take an adult education course in database maintenance, read a few books on the subject, or hire a computer consultant to go over your needs and then teach you how to apply technology to them.

Building a Database

I can't tell you how many times I've met with new clients who want to reach out to their contacts, and when we ask if they have an Excel list of their database or anything in place so we can effectively reach out to their customers, their answer is no. It's the 21st century, yet I've had 50-year old companies hand me file boxes and manila folders stuffed with business cards. But it's not just the companies that have been around for decades.

Even businesses that seem to be on the cutting edge have stunned me at times by their lack of database technology. In today's competitive climate, this just isn't an efficient way to handle business communications. So what happens is, instead of a half-hour task per week for someone within their organization to efficiently and effectively enter the information into a computerized system, it's now a taxing job that requires hours and hours of an employee's time to sort through and enter contact information. This causes most to say in frustration, "Oh, forget it" or "It's going to cost how much to do this?" My response is always the same: If you are not keeping contacts electronically these days, you are fighting an uphill battle. Because I can bet your competitors are.

If you recognize your own company here, don't worry—you can start today, right now, to build up a database and I assure you, this will become a priceless and highly effective marketing tool for your business for years.

So let's say you've collected a million business cards (okay, maybe a few thousand). What do you do with them? Rather than leaving them in your desk drawer or stuffed into your day planner bound with rubber bands in groups of 20, your first step should be to sort through them all and organize them in a way that is useful and meaningful to you. For example, you can create piles of files by industry, such as financial planners, accountants, or lawyers. You can organize them alphabetically or geographically. Choose whatever works best for your specific needs. Once that's done, create a contact database. Creating a contact database allows you to store all your contacts' information in one centralized location (not to mention, it also helps to de-clutter your life). It will help you to keep in touch with your contacts on a regular basis, it can be used as a tool for mining new business, and you can even use it as a networking tool to connect contacts to each other. You will literally have tons of important information right at your fingertips.

There are many options available to you, and just as you had to try on different networking groups, you may have to do some initial research on contact databases to find out which one works best for your specific needs. Here are some places to start:

Excel is the most basic way of keeping all your contacts in one place. Formatting is the most important step, so be sure to record the following information for all your contacts:

First Name
Middle Name
Last Name
Title
Company Name
Address
City
State
Zip
Phone
Fax
Email
Website
Notes/categories

The benefit of Excel is that it's quite easy and convenient to use, which is why so many businesspeople have embraced this option. It is simply a spreadsheet. You can import Excel files into many different applications including Outlook and Constant Contact or use your list to mail merge letters and labels in Microsoft Word (a PC application).

Outlook is great because it works with both your calendar and your e-mail accounts. You also have the option of writing additional information about the contact in a "notes" section. For instance, where you met the person, what they are looking for in terms of business and/or contacts, descriptions of services, and other unique, identifying information to help you remember who they are and what they need. You can also assign categories to each contact. You can set up reminders, which will automatically notify you when you need to call or e-mail them. I don't know of any Rolodex that can do that!

After you have created a contact database, upload your Excel file into a service such as Constant Contact (*www.constantcontact.com*). Constant Contact is simply e-mail marketing software that enables users to communicate with their contacts. For example, if you want to send a monthly newsletter to everyone in your networking group, you can do it through this system with one click of your mouse.

Once you've created your database and uploaded your Excel file into Constant Contact, you are then able to create separate and multiple lists, sorted by state and categories (which you name). People can "live" in separate lists so you can choose who to send specific information to. You can also search your contacts very easily by using multiple search terms, such as state, zip code, name, or category name. Although it's a bit tricky to keep your lists in multiple locations, you have the ability to export updated information out of Constant Contact to update your database whenever you want.

Mac users have different, yet equally suitable options. For example, Dave Goldberg, president of Digital Waterworx, a Long Island corporate communications production company, says the Apple Suite of Tools he uses has an address book application that works seamlessly with other organizational and mailing tools.

Maintain up-to-date information on your database once it's set up. My agency has worked with plenty of companies that don't have an up-to-date database, so when it comes time to do a direct mail campaign, an e-mail blast, or any sort of outreach to their current customers and/or potential customers, is overwhelming and extremely time consuming.

Once you have organized your databases, you'll find that sending out e-newsletters, or notes to specific groups of people, or following up on the "touch base" reminders that pop up on your computer, is a snap.

Business Card Holders

Once you create your computer databases, you may want to trash your business cards. And as you network, you should get into the practice of adding names to your databases immediately after meeting someone new. Throwing away the business card is your option. Personally, while I have a highly functional database file, I wouldn't be organized without my business card holders, too.

The way I remember people is by looking at their cards. I may not remember the person, or what they look like by looking at a long list of names, but you can bet when I open up my business card holder(s) that once I see their card, I see "them," no matter how long ago I met them. And that's why keeping actual business cards is key for me.

My cards aren't arranged by the person's name; rather they are arranged by industry. This way, if I'm looking for a moving company, I can look under "M" for all the moving companies that I know. And while I remember my contacts by category, not everyone is the same. Others may remember a company name, but not the person's name, so you file your business cards the way you see fit. I have dozens of business card holders and each one is sacred to me. Obviously, I update information periodically, tossing and updating cards, but for me, having both an electronic database and my cards at my fingertips works! And I am confident that I have a paper backup system in place, just in case.

Keeping Tabs on Your Networking Groups

Keeping track of all of the networking groups and organizations you join might seem like a daunting task. And in all honestly, it can get confusing at times. But here again, organizational skills come into play. To keep organized, I have separate notebooks for every one of my networking meetings and I take copious notes. I have binders for every group and I bring them with me and fill in what people want, who is doing what, and so on, so I can refer back to them. I also save my notes in a folder of who needs what and who wants what. I have a master calendar in Outlook that I use to track meetings. I have my notes section in Outlook where I keep notes. But here's one great tip: The very best way to keep track is to address a situation immediately. If someone in a group asks for something specific, that is my number-one concern for at least the next 48 hours. I get it done, and get it off my plate! So if you enter your new contacts into whatever system you have as you make the contacts, you will never feel overwhelmed or intimidated by keeping track.

Those who hold onto their cards and don't follow up promptly will later have a hard time staying in touch with their networks. It is a bit time consuming, but if you treat networking like you would any other business development activity for yourself, you will get the hang of it and it won't get out of control. Think of this as starting a business. You attack every request with an urgency to follow through, so you can move on with your own business needs.

In a nutshell, I have all sorts of ways to keep tabs on my networking group activities and requests, and I encourage you to find a system that works for your individual needs. Whatever system you use, you definitely need a system. You aren't going to be a networker without staying in touch with the people you meet and you aren't going to stay in touch with the people you meet without a system that's easy for you to use. Now, I'm an organized person by nature, and I understand fully that others may not have this characteristic. So if being organized eludes you, it's imperative that you hire someone you can work with, a personal organizer who understands whatever system you currently use—whether you are a pack rat, or a piler of papers, or someone who doesn't know how to keep track of your desktop and your files. It's the best money you will ever spend on yourself and your business.

As a Fast Track Networker, You Now Know:

- Mounds of accumulated business cards don't serve a good purpose. They need to be organized—add the names to a database. It may seem like a daunting task right now, and it will probably require a lengthy time commitment, but you must do it. Without computerized database systems in place, you are not working competitively and effectively.

- It's time to part with the Rolodex. There are too many excellent electronic systems available to continue using this relic.

- If you're uncertain how to set up an electronic database, calendar, and mailing systems, ask experts for help. The more you utilize these organized systems, the more adept you will become, so let go of the fear! And don't be alarmed if they require hours of labor (which you will have to pay for) to set you up. The results will be priceless and I assure you, you will be amazed at your efficiency from there on.

- A very useful backup system is to keep organized business card holders in addition to your electronic files. But don't just file them into their slots without any sense of order. File them by name, company, or by industry, so the information is always right at your fingertips.

- Organize your networking groups with binders, folders, files—whatever works best for your own needs. But you must have a system in place, or you will quickly become overwhelmed, which will paralyze any networking efforts you have already launched.

- If organization is not one of your strong points, or just the thought of straightening out your messy, paper-ridden desk makes you anxious, hire a professional organizer. You will be amazed at the quick results, and even if you feel you cannot maintain the systems they put into place, have them visit you on a regular basis (once a month, once a week) so that you can keep an orderly system in place.

Tossing out a Rolodex can be a cathartic experience. It signifies that one has joined the state-of-the-art! And there are so many efficient and better ways to maintain contact information.
—Marti Riedel, MA, LPC,
licensed professional counselor
Keller, Texas

Chapter Twelve

A Promise Is a Promise. Keep Yours.

Joining networking groups can be compared to signing up for a gym membership. People join gyms all the time with the intention of going, working out, losing weight, feeling better. They go for a month, maybe two. But when they aren't seeing the results that they either thought they were going to get or that they were promised by the buff guy at the front desk, they quit. They quit because they believe the effort they put in should yield the results that they visualized in their minds.

Unfortunately, I've seen that same short-sighted mentality many times when it comes to networking groups. Businesspeople join networking groups with the intention that they will attend, whether it's a weekly or monthly obligation. They have an expectation that they will go, achieve great results, make new contacts, obtain new clients, and their expectation is on target. They should be doing all of these things and reaping all of these rewards.

However, just like going to the gym and working out, sometimes results take a while. Like working out, the effort you put in is in direct proportion to what you get out. So if you are only showing up to your networking group with your business cards in hand, but nothing for the other members, guess what? You are definitely not going to get the results you want.

The Importance of Follow-Up

Having said that, I know tons of smart businesspeople who see the value in attending networking functions and in joining networking groups, and they do all of the things they are supposed to when it comes to getting out there. They make a point of being at these events regularly, of reaching out to others who are present and of forming the basis for productive alliances. But here's where so many of these savvy individuals err: They neglect to follow up. They mean to; good intentions are not the problem. The problem is without actual follow-up, the time and energy spent on meeting new contacts is worthless.

Consider this scenario: Susan, a realtor, attends a breakfast networking meeting where she encounters several professionals. One of them is Bob, who runs an ad agency. As the meeting comes to a close, Bob asks Susan to give him a call. Susan assures him that she will, but because she figures she doesn't know anyone who needs advertising, and because she thinks Bob probably won't help her grow out her business (after all, her firm has already embarked in an ad campaign), she neglects to follow up. A month passes, and Susan attends the next breakfast networking meeting, one she hopes Bob will skip, as she never called him. But Bob is a good business-man, so he does attend, and goes right up to Susan, to tell her she should have called him. Turns out Bob had a friend who was looking to purchase a house in Susan's territory. When she didn't call, Bob's friend signed up with another realtor. Susan didn't just lose a potential client in Bob's friend; she also lost something no amount of money can replace: her integrity. She said she'd call, and she didn't.

Committing to the Cause

Networking requires follow-up. It's that simple. That can mean calling someone you just met after they directly ask you to do so (like Bob), or following up on your own initiative. Networking also requires commitment, an agreement that you will do what you set out to do, or said you would do, within the time frame promised. You've indicated that you are on board. You have agreed that the commitment is doable, or at least you will give it your best shot. You've committed to someone or something and what you do next, and how you honor your commitments says a lot about you as a person and whether people can view you as someone they can count on both now and in the future.

People commit to things all the time in business, and in general, most are admirable and have the truest of intentions when they say they will do something or provide someone with a lead or a connection. But we've all had people fall short on their commitments, whether in our personal lives or our business lives, and when that happens, we are left with all sorts of feelings that range from frustration and bewilderment, to anger and often, resentment. Do we hold these people who committed accountable? Sometimes yes, but more often than not, especially in the world of business networking, we tend to write them off, at least in our minds, and move on. This is what Bob did to Susan.

Being There in Body, Mind, and Spirit

In order to make the most of networking group participation and to demonstrate to others your strong sense of commitment and responsibility, remember that you are there to participate. By participate, this means you are actively (or should be actively) thinking of the others in the group. What can you do for them? What is going to make a difference in their business growth and success? What did you promise to do for someone, and are you doing it?

Although you may be tempted to make other things in your life a priority, if you want to be successful at networking, never skip meetings. You have a commitment to show up! You are important to the dynamics of the group. Once your group has formed and gelled, when you don't show up, not only are you physically missed by others, but your energy is missed. The dynamics of the group shift and by you not being there, the group doesn't function as well as when you are there. There is usually time spent wondering where you are and what you are doing. There is a feeling of loss and a sense of disappointment, not to mention that it causes people to question your level of responsibility and commitment to the group and may lead them to wonder if you place the group (and them) lower on your list of priorities. Lastly, when you don't show up regularly, you are doing yourself a disservice by possibly missing out on important information that is discussed. And what if one of your group members brings leads for you and you're not there?

On the other hand, I know some networkers who do attend every single meeting and promise everyone in attendance the world. Although enthusiasm is a terrific asset, it's easy to get carried away with it at a networking event and perhaps "over-promise" in the quest to make a good impression on someone you have just met. So avoid offering to connect a new acquaintance with one of your contacts spontaneously. If you can't follow through, for whatever reason, you will be thought of as someone who is unreliable. But do put yourself out there whenever possible. For example, if you belong to a group that takes on other projects, whether to raise money for an organization, or organize events open to others, volunteer! Stand up and say, "I will take that on." Be visible in your group. The members of your group need to see you in action, so become active! Following are several examples of how being active can pay off.

I belong to a monthly networking group and when it was first in formation, the founder came to me and asked if we would develop a logo for the group. In return, she would promote us at the monthly meetings, on her Website, in her e-mail blasts, and wherever she could. I immediately jumped on this and we developed a great logo for her group. She was so pleased that she included my company name alongside the logo on her banner, which hangs at every meeting. She mentions us and thanks us by name at every meeting. As a result, we have received calls from members of the group asking for logo designs, in addition to the design of their marketing materials. So you can see what a smart decision it was for us to volunteer to create the logo for this networking group.

I am also involved in a local Women's Civitan Club. Civitans are known for their work in the community. They raise money for organizations, they volunteer to help at events when needed, and they are committed to going above and beyond for those who need help. When our group was first starting out, there were all sorts of chair positions available, all sorts of roles I could have volunteered for, but I took on the role of Project Chair. That means I am the person that other Civitan members come to with information on the projects they want to support and the organizations they want to support. At every weekly meeting, I am visible, as I get to stand in front of my group and tell them the different projects and programs that our group is involved with. I have contact with more than 80 women Civitans on a regular basis and these members get to see who I am in a leadership role. They see and hear my excitement as I speak to them about the projects we need their support with, they read my e-mails when I send out information (where my agency signature line and Web address are very visible), and they interact with me on a regular basis. Did I volunteer at Civitan because of business? No. I volunteered to be the Project Chair because I wanted to be involved, but in being involved, I also wanted to be visible. The role fills my heart with happiness, as I am contributing to my community through the good work that we do, but at the same time, it reinforces my agency's image, message, and theme with another whole group of people!

Here's another example: There is a not-for-profit organization on Long Island, New York, called the Long Island Way. It was started by a very smart and enterprising woman by the name of Donna Cariello. This is a group that brings for-profit companies together with not-for-profit agencies for the betterment of both. It's an amazing organization that continues to grow and flourish, and for two years, my agency did all their PR and marketing at no charge. But we were connected to all sorts of businesses within our target market that were aware that we did the PR and marketing work for the Long Island Way. The not-for-profits were simultaneously aware that we did this work, as we were highlighted in all sorts of material that was distributed by Donna. You see, this made us extremely visible.

Now, some of you may be reading this and thinking "Yeah, but with a marketing/PR machine in place, what do I do if I'm an accountant, attorney, window washer, dog walker, acting coach, manufacturer, or just plain old me looking for a new career?" My answer to you is: think outside the box and think about what you could do for your organization or group. I know a woman who is in the real estate industry. She doesn't do PR and marketing, yet she is the one who always raises her hand and volunteers to be a greeter at the door of all the mixers/events she attends. She puts herself in the middle of the event as the hostess. She created this job for herself, and rather than acting as the hostess of the event, she actually is!

A businessman I know who owns an insurance agency is always the first in my group to offer his office number to field calls from prospective members who want to attend as guests at the networking group. He gets dozens of calls every month from people who hear "Good Morning, Jim White Insurance, can I help you?" This is incredible reinforcement of his agency name, building on capturing what I call top of mind presence in the community. Now, out of those dozen calls, many won't do anything other than ask when the next networking meeting is, but if Jim is doing this right (and he is), he is visible in other ways within the community. When people see or hear his name somewhere else, or meet him for the first or second time, they think "Hey, I know you. I called your office to inquire about the networking meeting." He is building his reputation in the community as part of a bigger circle than just an insurance salesperson.

Suppose you are an accountant within a larger firm. You probably have a conference room of sorts. People who belong to groups/organizations/associations who have access to a meeting or conference room are golden! Offer it up and make it available to your group for meetings. There is nothing better than meeting where you work. Here's why: There are a couple of law firms I am aware of that always offer their conference room for meetings. When you meet there, not only are there pens/pencils available with their name imprinted on them, but the pads they offer you to take notes on for your meeting have their name, logo, phone number, and Website emblazed across the top. Of course, you take the pad and pen with you when you go—what better brand enhancement could they ask for? They don't offer free legal advice to the group members, they don't "do" anything that directly corresponds to their line of work, but they offer something of value and then brand the heck out of who they are and what they do while you are in their office!

"Commitment is what transforms a promise into a reality." This quote, attributed to Abraham Lincoln, perhaps says it all. But what you personally do each time you make a commitment (each time you promise to make an introduction, every time you volunteer to help out with a fundraiser, every organization that you join) says volumes about you as a person. Sure, it's easy to make a commitment. But what that entails is what really counts (the follow up) and what people will remember the next time they are looking for someone that they can truly count on to get the job done.

Finally, as someone who's been successfully networking for so many years, I'm often asked if I keep track of who I connect with whom. While I don't keep formal notes, in the back of my mind, I'm always aware of the people I've connected. And it's the people that follow up with me and say thank you who remain top of mind for me.

I might easily forget about those who don't take the time out to acknowledge or express gratitude when I introduce them to one of my connections. I've had that happen a dozen and one times where all of a sudden, I find out that Jim is doing work for George and getting tons of business because I put them together, and neither one of them picks up the phone to say thanks. The best way to handle this is to pick up the phone and call George and Jim and tell them that you heard about their mutual success and let them know that you are happy that they connected and explain that you love to know about success stories, that you like to know when things work out between people that you have put together. Tell them that you would love to know of others that you have introduced them to that have worked out. This outreach to them accomplishes two things. First, it puts you back in touch with your contact (and remember it's important to stay in touch with the people in your network). Second, it shows both George and Jim that you care about them, that you care about your network, and that you don't want to just be a referral source, but that you want to be a part of their business growth and success. So let them know you care and also let them know that it's important to you to know when you've done something significant for them!

Thanking the people who helped you, or tried to help you (even if the connection didn't pan out), is an important part of network follow-up. Remember, your reputation is at stake with every business move you make, or don't make, for that matter.

As a Fast Track Networker, You Now Know:

- Joining a networking group is only part of your success. The other part is following up on what you say and do at the meetings you attend.
- If you don't follow through with a request or a promise, your integrity will be compromised. And it's possible that a great potential connection will not want to network with you again if they are let down.
- When you join a group, you must commit to attending each and every single networking meeting. Otherwise, the group dynamics will change. You will be missed by other attendees. You will

miss out on important shared information. You may even miss out on leads that members are bringing you.

- Volunteering for networking group activities is a great way to show that you are a dynamic individual. However, don't get carried away and commit to things that you can't possibly do. Keep yourself in check and its fine to say, "I'll get back to you on that." But if you do say that, make sure you get back to them, regardless of your response!

- Showing gratitude by thanking people when they share their contacts with you is part of following up. Even if a connection doesn't necessarily work out, call the person who gave you the initial contact to acknowledge their efforts. By expressing gratitude, you are building a great reputation for yourself.

I can't count the number of times that I go to networking events where people say 'Oh, you should talk to so and so. I'll send you his contact information tomorrow' and yet they never do. What are these people thinking? I wonder if they realize that the next time I see them at an event, I will steer clear of them... Why tell someone you will do something and then not do it? It's beyond me.

—Rebecca Sands, student
New Paltz, New York

Chapter Thirteen

Putting the *Strategic* in Strategic Alliances

Whether you are looking to share risk, resources, or your company needs to grow and develop in ways that it couldn't on its own. Strategic alliances are different than just networking relationships, although most of the successful ones I've seen and participated in have come from effective networking.

Strategic alliances allow one company to tap into the strengths of another without the legal, financial, and cultural complications that often accompany a merger or acquisition. They are also fluid—easy to start, easy to get out of. The beauty of this is that you can form a strategic alliance with another company for just one or two projects, or for years.

Getting an edge on a highly competitive marketplace is usually the reason that people form a strategic alliance. For example, if you are a one-person public relations firm and see that other PR companies around you are offering graphic design as a benefit to working with them, you may want to form a strategic alliance with a graphic design firm, or a graphic artist, as well. By doing so, you will have a practical resource at your fingertips when a client requests design work; at the same time, the graphic design firm you have formed an alliance with could easily refer business to you, when one of their clients needs PR services.

First Steps

So, where do you start? How do you take your business from small- to medium-sized or medium-sized to large, with whom, or to which marketplace? You may think this is too difficult and time consuming, and that may be the case. However, the benefits can be wholly worth your efforts. So here's how to do it.

One of the first steps you need to take in order to find a good strategic alliance is to do a great deal of research. This is where your networking skills will be put to the test, as now is the time when you need to attract businesspeople who share your values and work ethics. There are many people in the business world who don't walk their talk, who may have a good show, but not a lot of follow through, so if you are looking for a strong alliance, these types of people are not going to be your best choice. Instead, look at your lists of contacts. Check your inner circle of 10, and your outer circle of 20. These are all people you've networked with, or are currently networking with. You know they are solid, that they have excellent reputations and that they follow through.

In addition to going through your lists of contacts, remember to continually expand your connections, so attend new networking event and meetings. You have to "get out, to get in"—that means if you aren't networking, if you aren't out there, it's going to be tough for you to know your choices of partners outside of the people you already work with. That's why the first step in developing any sort of strategic alliance is to understand what/who you are looking for and where you are going to find them.

Let's say you are a residential real estate company owner. Who would be your best strategic partners? Obviously one would be a mortgage broker. Maybe one would be an insurance sales person. There would be quite a few. I know a mortgage broker in Albuquerque who has built an incredible strategic alliance with people that can all work together. In order to accomplish this, her very first steps were to go to every event and every networking function she read about. She joined all the industry groups and met everyone she targeted, so she could find the very best partners with whom to form strategic alliances. Her name is Melinda and I'm going to refer to her as we move along.

Stipulate Goals and How to Meet Them

The next step is to be clear about your desired outcome. Be as specific as possible and identify exactly what your goals are with a strategic alliance. Specify how much you want your connection to grow together, the number of hours you can commit to working on your project and the other commitments that may affect your business or financial situations. Think about any fears you might have about forming this new business relationship. You will be investing valuable time, as well as valuable money, so consider what might happen if this new alliance doesn't work out.

I've witnessed many strategic partnerships fail because of a lack of communication. Here's just one example: Two businessmen that I know, one in banking and one in business management, decided to start a family-owned business network/organization. It was a great idea, but they both thought that what they brought to the table was the most important aspect to the alliance. The banker thought that his contacts were vital and that filling a room was all he needed to do. The management consultant thought that because he knew the internal business and emotional aspects of being in a family-owned business that was enough. This really was a brilliant concept, but unfortunately, they never thought beyond the idea of both of them shining in their own light. They launched the group, many people came to the meeting, and many of them wanted to join. There was talk about various companies sponsoring the group, yet after one meeting, the group died, never to meet again. Why? Because the banker and the management consultant never talked about the time it would take after the meeting to sign these people up, nor about who was going to do the administrative work, who was going to handle member relations, and what was going to happen next. So although they had the makings of a great initial strategic partnership, what they really had was a one-shot wonder idea and no plan to move it forward. A strategic partnership is, in fact, a new business, a new venture, a new market to go after, and it needs to be treated as such. You wouldn't start a business without a plan, right? So why involve someone else, or another company in a strategic alliance, without a complete plan?

Melinda on the other hand, was very clear about her strategic partnership goals. She knew she wanted to work with the best of the best, and after she identified them, she got them all together in a room and laid out her plan to form an alliance (which she named The Albuquerque Relocation Group). She also explained how they would succeed.

Communicate Everything

Many business alliances fail because assumptions are made—and those assumptions are usually incorrect. This happens because of a lack of or just poor communication. Every single detail regarding your alliance must be addressed in order to avoid misunderstandings and problems. Clarify everything. Don't be afraid to state the obvious, because what is obvious to you may not be to the other person. Take notes. Confirm everything in writing, as soon as possible after you meet and get firm commitments from all parties involved.

Sometimes, we have a "we can do it all attitude," so we may enter into a partnership or a project without having the details, without having the communication, and without knowing key issues up front. We take it on, we believe we can do it all, and we overlook the details or the other person's lack of doing what we thought they would do. So to compensate, we try to take care of it ourselves and somewhere down the road, an uncomfortable feeling begins to take shape. That usually means we feel we are being taken advantage of, and resentment may build up. When that happens, it's your fault. It's not your partner's fault that you took it all on and now feel resentment. Most people are happy to let another do all the work and they take whatever benefit they can. So, if you are one of these "bring it on" people, stop now. Communicate your expectations. Draw out clear details of who is going to do what, and stick to them. Have weekly meetings with your partner and go over what has been done, who did it, and what needs to be accomplished in the next week. Remember, its business, not personal.

Melinda's second meeting with the people who agreed to be a part of the Albuquerque Relocation Group was a success, and the group started meeting on a regular basis. They communicated up front with each other about what they were willing to bring to the table, what kind of time commitment they could give, what kinds of resources they had, and what they were willing and able to do. They wrote it down, and they all agreed on specific tasks at hand.

Set Specific Deadlines

Set specific time lines, trial time frames, and deadlines for whatever needs to get accomplished. Many people agree in principal to something, and then find that due to prior commitments or unexpected events, they can't honor their agreements. By setting trial time frames, you can get an idea of your partner's management style, attention to detail, and your partner's actual investment in the project (time, resources, and money). Remember always to include a time frame for task completion. One way to do this is by setting stages to every task: Agree to stage one. Based on the results of stage one, proceed to stage two, and so on. But don't be tempted to take the project beyond stage one until you have seen and realized your partner's true commitment. If your partner misses the first deadline, will your partner miss future deadlines?

I'm a "get it done" person. I've never waited until the last minute to take care of things that need to be taken care of. And when I enter into any sort of relationship, I try to under-promise, but over-deliver. However, I also have no concept of time and I think everything should take five minutes. Not everyone is like that. I know it now, but I didn't always—and it used to be very difficult for me to find strategic partners. When I did, I would get extremely frustrated. I would feel like I was the one taking on the entire project, and the reason was because there were no time frames set forth. There wasn't a clear understanding of who was going to do what and when they were going to do it!

I'll give you an unfortunate example. A few years ago, a woman I knew came to me with an idea for a strategic partnership. As the owner of a local security company, she wanted to orchestrate a large-scale "Security Forum" on Long Island—bringing in a number of experts to address different aspects of security (home, business, identity theft, and so on). I thought it was a great idea—and heightened concerns about security in recent years and the fact that nothing like this had been done on Long Island made it an even greater idea. I thought, "This is great. She has the knowledge, she has the peer connections, and she has great insight into this venture." So without taking the time to fully draw up the plan about what each other's expectations were, I had my agency dive in. We created a name and a logo for the symposium. I had my assistant spend hours and hours compiling a targeted sponsor mailing list. We developed an initial brochure and a Website so we could start marketing the project.

Then I asked the security company owner for an analysis of how she visualized the breakout/speaking sessions that were to be held during the symposium. I asked once and got no response. I asked twice and received a promise that she would send it to me. Meanwhile, my agency kept moving forward. I found a center that would host this for us. They requested a $5,000 deposit, but my "strategic partner" didn't want to put up the money. She finally sent me the list of speakers she thought would work for the event. We kept moving ahead. We finalized the letter to send to the potential speakers, asking them to participate, and I began asking for contacts within her world to talk to about sponsorships.

Again, I had to wait a long time for her response. Finally, she said she would contact them. A week, two weeks, three weeks passed. On and on, my agency continued doing much of the work required in order to move ahead, with her not doing much at all. Finally, we got together, and I said, "It doesn't feel like you are actively involved in this project." Her answer to me was, "I brought you the idea, and I don't really have time to do much more." Well, that wasn't a strategic partnership. That was a total misunderstanding and non-communicating of who was going to do what and what the expectations were as we went along.

I've watched Melinda's group. With their plan and with their vision, they are attacking the residential real estate market in Albuquerque with such fervor, enthusiasm, and cooperation that there is no way they aren't going to succeed.

Exit Gracefully

When forming your alliance, make sure you stipulate exit clauses. It's much more preferable to lose a partner in the early stages, than to lose your good name over time. Sometimes differing styles of management and leadership create disharmony. Or what initially seems to be a small annoyance may become a serious irritation later. For example, you may form a partnership with someone who is always a half hour late. You, on the other hand, are always prompt. You may initially laugh at your partner's lateness, but after a few months of always waiting for her, it may become really annoying! More importantly, it may hamper the way your strategic alliance is working on a day-to-day basis, which would affect it negatively in the long term.

Be Positive, But Consider Both Sides of the Coin

Although your aim is to create a strong alliance, before confirming anything, brainstorm on the best- and worst-case scenarios regarding this partnering. Think about the worst thing that can happen and what you will to do if that happens. Our worst case with the Security Forum was going to be spending all the money on the place, the printing, the time devoted by my employees and then not having any attendees. I should have noticed the red flag waving in my face when she didn't want to put up her share of the deposit for the rental of the space. So if an alliance is not based on a win-win goal, it has little chance of success. Without a win-win approach understood by both sides, one partner is likely to become frustrated, annoyed, reluctant, and eventually resentful of always being on the short end of the stick.

Celebrate Success

People are so busy doing, doing, doing that they forget to stop and celebrate their successes in life. When there are budget constraints, we often think we can't afford to celebrate as lavishly as we would like, so we don't do anything at all. But in order to maintain your own motivation and your partner's, it's important to record the milestones in your alliance. Your first order, your first check, are typically shared achievements that deserve recognition. Celebrations of shared achievements build the relationships. I had a very strong strategic alliance with a woman who started out as the major gifts cultivator at a not-for-profit. The first time she brought the agency a client, I cut her a finder's fee check and she thanked me and we went on our way. The second time she brought me a client, I cut her a finder's fee check and then we went to lunch to talk about this relationship and if we could go further. She told me she always had wanted to start an event management company, but couldn't really afford to quit her job at the moment. So together, we came up with a two-year plan where she would come to work for me, bring in business, and we would launch a division of my agency that would be owned by both of us for five years. At the end of five years, it would be hers and hers alone, but with me getting some of the profit. It worked. It was amazing. We took the time to talk. We took the time to devise a plan. We were very clear about who was going to do what and how we were going to do this. And we always celebrated our successes, which fueled us for what had to be accomplished next.

Starting the Process

Of all the people you know personally, have read about in books, magazines, or seen in the media—which two people would be perfect to start a strategic partnership with? You may have to do some research to find contact details, but it's worth the effort.

Do your homework, do a SWOT (Strengths, Weaknesses, Opportunities, and Threats) analysis, highlighting the positives and negatives of a joint alliance, and prepare a plan. Write a proposal which includes all the information that your potential partner will need in order to make a decision. Next, make the phone call and make contact.

Fear of Failure

It's quite common for business people to avoid forming strategic alliances for fear of failure. After all, it's one thing to attempt a new marketing campaign for your own business. If it fails, you take full responsibility and move on. It's entirely another experience to try a new venture with another person. You have the best intentions. Your partner in a strategic alliance has the best intentions and yet, for one reason or another, things may not work out. Most of the time, it's due to communication or lack thereof. A strategic partnership is very similar to a partnership in work and in your personal life. You are investing time, energy, effort, and oftentimes money, so when there is a breakdown in one of these areas, most of the time, resentment starts to set in. If you don't talk about how you are feeling right away, it will get worse. So, if you can nip whatever issue is happening right then and there, you may be able to continue on your path together. And what if it just doesn't work? Sometimes you can go back to just a networking relationship, and that's like getting married or engaged, and then trying to go back to being just friends if it doesn't work. That can be challenging. So, you may have to be the bigger person, especially if your networking relationship was good and you want it to continue. But keep this in mind: chances are, if you are feeling like the strategic alliance wasn't working the way you wanted to, or the way you hoped it would, the other person was feeling it as well.

Being fearful of something not working out isn't a good reason to not try it. One of my favorite quotes in the whole world is, "What would you attempt to do if you knew you couldn't fail?" I have this on a paperweight on my desk and I read it every single day. I think it is a great reminder to go for it, to try new things, to explore new relationships, to do things differently because doing things the same way every day is boring. Networking relationships sometimes don't work out, but that doesn't mean you failed. It means it didn't work out. That doesn't mean you give up. Partnerships and strategic partnerships sometimes fail, too.... Keep on moving!

We can find excuses every day to stay in our comfort zones and not approach others who can help us grow our businesses and our careers, yet if we have courage, we can overcome rejection and pursue our dreams, goals, and targets through strategic alliances with others. Remember, no man (or woman) is an island! That holds true in our personal lives and our business lives.

As a Fast Track Networker, You Now Know:

- Strategic alliances are fluid and they can help you move your business forward in new and exciting directions.
- Network with people who will be strong partners—those should be business people who share your work ethics and values.
- Write down your goals in a strategic alliance, but don't stop there. Communicate every detail regarding your alliance, how you will work together, who will be responsible for which tasks, and follow through consistently.
- Set time lines and deadlines and test them out to make sure you and your partner are always on the same page.
- Formulate an exit plan in case your alliance does not work out. Get out while you are ahead, rather than when your reputation or finances are in ruins.

- Remember to celebrate your successes, large and small. This will keep you motivated as you move forward with your plans.
- Don't allow fear of failure to stop you from forming a strategic alliance. Failure is usually due to poor or lack of communication. And even if your alliance does not work, you can learn valuable lessons from it and move on. So do not let that stop you.

Every entrepreneur should be forced to put together a strategic alliance. Even if it doesn't work out, it's an incredible learning experience for all parties involved. You learn what to do and what not to do. And, you learn perhaps the most important business lesson of all—to take some calculated risks.

—Molly Massen, retail therapy provider,
Owner of Substance of Taos
Taos, New Mexico

Resources

Associations and Organizations

AssociationsUnlimited.com: A database that has more than 46,000 international, U.S., national, regional, state and local not for profit organizations.

Weedles Guide to Associations (*www.weedles.com/associations*): Just as fabulous in terms of seeking organization and association information, but unlike AssociationsUnlimited.com, it's FREE!

Online Communities

www.imantri.com: an online peer-to-peer community that offers mentoring and coaching. This is a great site because it facilitates connections between members, and there is no cost to job seekers.

www.fastcompany.com/company-of-friends.com: *Fast Company* magazine's global network of fans. Great place to connect with some of the very best in forward thinkers and people that have made up their own job descriptions based on their interests, skills, and creative thinking.

www.delphiforums.com: A member-managed online community. Members can build, manage, and grow their own on-line communities.

www.ecademy.com: Ecademy believes networking and a philosophy of winning by sharing are keys to success. Membership is free.

www.jigsaw.com: An online business contact marketplace where marketers, recruiters, and others can buy, sell, and trade business contact information. Jigsaw offers members access to an online database of accurate corporate contact information.

www.linkedin.com: LinkedIn allows you to see the whole network of people you can reach through your trusted friends, and search for the contacts you need to get more business done. This is a great online networking tool. Your friends are able to introduce you to their friends and they introduce you to the people you want to contact. Less than six degrees of separation on Linkedin.com.

www.meetup.com: Online organizers create events, outings, and get-togethers for anyone who wants to participate. There is a meet-up group for virtually every interest you can think of, and if there isn't, you can start one! Great place to highlight your local networking group or job-seekers group.

www.workster.com: This site specializes in building college networks that are exclusive. Through these networks, members get connected to career opportunities. No cost to job seekers.

www.networkingforprofessionals.com: An online networking group designed for professionals, where you can build your business, improve your client base, and/or advance your career. There is a fee to join.

www.realcontacts.com: Worldwide online employment service.

www.Ryze.com: More than 500,000 members in more than 200 countries, Ryze allows you to create a networking-oriented home page and send messages to other members. You can join special networks related to your industry, interest, or location.

www.Tribe.net: A service that allows you to not only create your own "tribe" around interest areas, but also receive recommendations of just about any kind.

www.thevirtualhandshake.com: A leading resource for users of technologies such as blogs, social network sites, virtual communities, and more. A great resource for learning more about building relationships online. No fee to join.

www.xing.com: Eight million members worldwide, committed to powering relationships based on trust for all professional people.

www.ziggs.com: Offers a search platform for finding more than 2.6 million public profiles from more than 66,000 companies.

www.zoominfo.com: A business information search engine, with profiles on more than 45 million people. In-depth information on industries, companies, people, products, services, and jobs. Job-seekers can post/edit free profiles, which can include your professional career details, bio, education, affiliations, and contact information.

Social Networking Websites

www.linkedin.com: See previous description.

www.facebook.com: The premiere social networking site that allows you to connect with friends, friends of friends, and friends of the friends of the friends. You can promote what you are doing, what you want to do, share photos, links, videos, and more.

www.squiddo.com: Showcase your expertise in one or more areas by creating knowledge pages called lenses. Using this site gives you an opportunity to showcase your knowledge, as well as link and promote yourself and your site.

www.digg.com: A social news sharing site for people to discover and share content from the Web. Members refer something (a Website, blog entry, video) to the community. Others in the community rate the entry with "digs." The more votes an entry receives, the higher it moves up, sometimes ending up on the site's front page.

www.del.icio.us.com: This social bookmarking site is a place to share your personal bookmarks with an entire community of others—and where you can see what other sites other people are bookmarking.

www.Twitter.com: A social networking site that allows you to tell people what you are doing right now. Postings are called "Tweets."

Job Clubs and Job Search Support

www.job-hunt.org: Allows you to search state by state for the job of your dreams.

www.executivesnetwork.com: A national peer-to-peer network for executives in a job search.

www.thefiveoclockclub.org: A members-only organization that is a national outplacement and career counseling network.

www.therileyguide.com: The go-to source for everything job related. A top rated site for job search and occupational information.

School Alumni Networking Groups

www.alumni.net: Offers links to high schools and colleges located in the United States and throughout the world.

www.classmates.com: High schools, colleges, military, and workplace databases.

www.reunion.com: Alumni of any American high school can visit this site and register, update information, search for old classmates, and re-connect.

Finding People on the Internet

When you want to network with someone or re-connect with someone that you've lost touch with, these sites have been cited among the best people search engines available.

- *www.pipi.com*
- *www.google.com*
- *www.facebook.com*
- *www.spock.com*
- *www.123people.com*
- *www.peoplespot.com*

Entrepreneurial Women's Organizations

- The National Association of Women Business Owners: *www.nawbo.org*
- Women on The Fast Track: *www.womenonthefasttrack.com*
- National Association for Female Executives: *www.nafe.com*
- The National Federation of Business and Professional Women: *www.bpwfoundation.com*
- Women President's Organization: *www.womenpresidentsorg.com*

Networking Groups Open to Both Men and Women

- BNI—The world's largest networking organization. Chapters in virtually every city: *www.bni.com*
- LeTip—Purpose is to exchange business leads, ideas and resources: *www.letip.com*
- No networking groups where you live? Check out: *www.Meetingsandmixers.com*—a national calendar of events, happenings, mixers and expos.

Thank you to Quintessential Careers (*www.quintcareers.com*), one of the Web's most comprehensive career sites for assistance in compiling these resources.

Index

About the Authors

Lucy Rosen is the Chief Solutions Officer of SmartMarketing Solutions, Inc., a leading marketing, public relations, and business development firm with offices in New York and New Mexico. A visionary in creating and expanding business opportunities for her clients (as well as others she just happens to meet) through her expertise in building strategic alliances, she is also the founder and president of Women on The Fast Track, a unique international networking organization for business women.

In 2005, Lucy was inducted into the Long Island Business News "Top 50 Women on Long Island" Hall of Fame, having won this distinction for three prior years. She has also been honored with the prestigious 2006 "Pathfinder Award" for a Woman In Business, given in recognition of her contributions to the local business community on Long Island.

Lucy has been a mentor and a member of the United States Small Business Administration Advisory Services Department for Women, as well as having been a developing member of the New York City Comptroller Department of Economic Development Task Force for Women and served on the Board of Directors of the New York City Chapter of the National Association of Women Business Owners, The Albuquerque Chapter of Albuquerque Women in Communications, The Albuquerque Women's Civitan Club, and the Women's Financial Group in New York.

A frequent speaker at groups across the country on a variety of business topics, Lucy is most happy when she is connecting others and helping them achieve their goals!

Award winning freelance journalist, editor, and author **Claudia Gryvatz Copquin** is a frequent contributor to the Pulitzer Prize-winning newspaper *Newsday*. She's also been published in *The New York Times*, *The L.A. Times*, and a slew of newspapers across the country. Her first non-fiction book, *The Neighborhoods of Queens* (Yale University Press, November 2007), which features an introduction by renowned historian Ken Jackson, was reviewed favorably twice by *The New York Times*. In addition, she's written hundreds of magazine features on family, parenting, business, lifestyle, and bridal. She is currently freelance associate editor of *Long Island Parent* magazine and is the founder/editor of *www.GettingMarriedonLongIsland.com*. Born in Buenos Aires, Argentina, Copquin is fluent in Spanish. She's a long-standing member of the Society of Professional Journalists as well as the Authors Guild.